IN HARM'S
WAY

IN HARM'S WAY

WAY

THE SINKING OF THE USS *INDIANAPOLIS*
AND THE STORY OF ITS SURVIVORS

An adaptation for young readers

DOUG STANTON AND
MICHAEL J. TOUGIAS

SQUARE
FISH

Henry Holt and Company
New York

An imprint of Macmillan Publishing Group, LLC
120 Broadway, New York, NY 10271 • mackids.com

Square Fish and the Square Fish logo are trademarks of Macmillan and are used by
Henry Holt and Company under license from Macmillan.

Our books may be purchased in bulk for promotional, educational, or
business use. Please contact your local bookseller or the Macmillan
Corporate and Premium Sales Department at (800) 221-7945 ext. 5442
or by email at MacmillanSpecialMarkets@macmillan.com.

Library of Congress Control Number: 2021916952

Originally published in the United States by Henry Holt and Company
First Square Fish edition, 2023
Book designed by Liz Dresner
Square Fish logo designed by Filomena Tuosto
Printed in the United States of America by Lakeside Book Company,
Harrisonburg, Virginia

ISBN 978-1-250-90934-3
10 9 8 7 6 5 4 3 2 1

AR: 7.2 / LEXILE: 970L

To history buff George Roux and his family—MT

~

In memory of the service and sacrifice of the USS Indianapolis
crew and family members

And my father, Derald Stanton, U.S. Army;
and my uncles, Milton Stanton, U.S. Navy;
Clifford "Kip" Earnest, U.S. Army; and
Norman Earnest, U.S. Navy—DS

CONTENTS

Introduction: Crew Members, Rescuers ix

PART I

1 The USS *Indianapolis* and Her Secret Cargo.......... 1
2 Information Withheld... 9
3 Torpedoes Fired 20

PART II

4 Fires Spreading.. 35
5 Abandon Ship!... 44
6 Radio Messages Ignored...................................... 55
7 Survivors, Drifting Apart 66
8 Is There a Doctor?... 75
9 Bumps in the Water... 84
10 Shark Attacks 94
11 Deadly Assumptions and
     a Deadly Temptation 101

12 Delirium Ignites Violence 111

13 Hallucinations in Full Boil 118

14 Father Conway and Captain Parke 128

PART III

15 Peleliu Island and Hope From Above 139

16 Supplies Falling From the Sky 147

17 The First Rescue 156

18 Ships Arrive 165

19 From One Kind of Fear to Another 173

20 Recovery 181

Epilogue 191

A Note From Doug Stanton 207

The USS *Indianapolis*/Gwinn "Angel" Scholarship 215

Glossary 216

Michael J. Tougias's Books 221

Bibliography 223

INTRODUCTION

The sinking of the USS *Indianapolis* was the worst naval disaster at sea in U.S. history. On July 30, 1945, near the end of World War II, the *Indianapolis* was torpedoed by a Japanese submarine. An estimated 300 men were killed upon impact and close to 900 others were cast into the Pacific Ocean. These survivors struggled to stay alive in a shark-filled sea. By the time help arrived—nearly four days and nights later—only 316 men were still alive.

KEY CREW MEMBERS OF USS *INDIANAPOLIS* (IN THE ORDER IN WHICH THEY ARE FIRST MENTIONED IN THE BOOK)

- Captain Charles McVay
- Marine Private Giles McCoy
- Dr. Lewis Haynes
- Father Thomas Conway

- Ensign Harlan Twible
- Chief Engineer Richard Redmayne
- Damage Control Officer K. C. Moore
- Officer of the Deck Lieutenant John Orr
- Quartermaster Bob Gause
- Radio Technician Jack Miner
- Marine Captain Edward Parke
- Sailor Bob Brundige

KEY MEN IN SURVIVORS' GROUPS

- Group #1: Dr. Haynes, Edward Parke, Father Conway, Bob Gause
- Group #2: Harlan Twible, Richard Redmayne, Jack Miner
- Group #3: Giles McCoy, Bob Brundige, Ed Payne, Willis Gray, Felton Outland
- Group #4: Captain McVay, Vincent Allard, John Spinelli

RESCUERS
Aviators and their planes:

- Lieutenant Chuck Gwinn (PV1 *Gambler 17*)
- Lieutenant Commander George Atteberry (Ventura bomber)

- Lieutenant Adrian Marks (PBY, nicknamed *Playmate 2*. PBY is an amphibious aircraft: *P* for Patrol, *B* for Bomber, *Y* for Navy code designation of Consolidated Aircraft manufacturer)
- Lieutenant Richard Alcorn (PBY)

Rescue ships:

- Destroyer escorts USS *Cecil J. Doyle* and USS *Dufilho*
- Destroyers USS *Ralph Talbot* and USS *Madison*
- Transport ships USS *Ringness*, USS *Bassett*, and USS *Register*

PART I

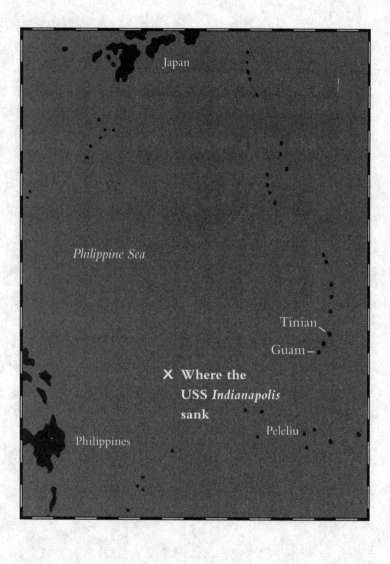

THE USS *INDIANAPOLIS* AND HER SECRET CARGO

Navy Captain Charles McVay stood on the bridge of his ship, forty-five feet above the main deck of the USS *Indianapolis*. Here he could monitor the navigation and communications equipment that his more seasoned sailors used in this cramped control room. The captain had safely guided his ship from San Francisco across much of the Pacific Ocean and was now approaching the tiny island of Tinian just north of Guam.

McVay's responsibilities, which were enormous, included the welfare of the 1,195 men on the ship (including the captain) and their readiness for battle. The average age of the crew was just nineteen, and many had little experience aboard a ship. For some of these young men, this was their first time away from home.

At forty-six years of age, the blue-eyed McVay was liked and respected by the sailors he commanded. He was a leader who went out of his way to be friendly to his men. When new crew members came aboard he made an effort to greet them by name, saying "Welcome, sailor. We're going to have a happy cruise."

McVay had served with distinction in the navy for many years and had experience aboard twelve different ships as he was steadily promoted to greater leadership roles. He had also been awarded the Silver Star just a few months earlier for actions he had taken while serving as executive officer aboard the cruiser *Cleveland* in the battle of the Solomon Islands.

The *Indianapolis*, often referred to as simply the *Indy*, was McVay's first assignment as captain when he took command of the ship in November 1944.

The *Indy* was in the naval classification of "cruiser" and was 610 feet long. In battle formation, cruisers flanked and protected the larger and less nimble battleships. Her main job was to shoot antiaircraft fire at enemy planes and protect the battleships, but she could also perform shore bombardments and sink enemy vessels. Smaller ships called destroyers were at the outer ring of the battle formation. Their responsibilities included prowling the edges of the entire flotilla to hunt down enemy subs that might threaten both the battleships and the cruisers.

While the *Indianapolis* was a killing war machine, the ship was also similar to a small town. The vessel had a medical section called a sick bay, and a mess hall where hungry sailors gathered to eat, and a jail called a brig. McVay was in charge of it all. His job was to make sure each man knew exactly what was expected of him while the ship was underway or in battle.

The captain could now see the island of Tinian, looking like a dot on the blue horizon. Tinian was a small but important island. From its airfield, giant B-29 bombers took off for raids over Japan.

McVay would soon order his men to drop anchor and he would wait for a barge to come out to the ship. Then he would oversee the unloading of a secret cargo onto the barge. Only a handful of men on the ship knew that the cargo contained the components for an atomic bomb, which would later be the first nuclear weapon ever used in war.

Knowing the cargo would soon be off-loaded, McVay hoped to receive authorization to get his men the gunnery practice they needed, and then proceed toward Japan to fight in the war.

Now, as the captain stood on the bridge, his feet spread wide as the ship rolled beneath him, he felt a sense of accomplishment that the first part of his mission was almost completed. He might have reflected back to the start of this particular assignment, and perhaps to the start of the war itself. After all, World War II had consumed the last three and a half years of McVay's life.

~

World War II began when Nazi Germany invaded Poland in 1939 and Great Britain and France tried to halt the Nazi takeover of Europe. At that time the U.S. had not joined in the war. But that changed when Imperial Japan bombed the U.S. naval base at Pearl Harbor, Hawaii, in a surprise attack on December 7, 1941. Much of the American battleship fleet was destroyed. Immediately after the bombing of Pearl Harbor, Germany, Italy, and Japan (the Axis powers) all declared war on the U.S., and the U.S. responded by declaring war on them.

Prior to the bombing of Pearl Harbor, tensions had been mounting between the U.S. and the Japanese. Like Germany, Japan had been aggressively expanding its control over neighboring countries, such as parts of China and French Indochina (Vietnam, Laos, and Cambodia). The U.S., along with the Dutch and British, responded with an oil embargo. This was a serious blow to Japan, which imported 90 percent of its oil. Without enough oil to fuel its planes, tanks, battleships, and troop support equipment, Japan's military would be crippled.

Despite the embargo, however, Japan refused to withdraw its troops from countries it had invaded.

Japanese leaders determined the embargo was unacceptable and that sooner or later war with the U.S. would break out. They decided that to win a war with the U.S. their best chance would be to strike first in a surprise attack.

After the bombing of Pearl Harbor, Japan was successful in taking over the Philippines and various French, Dutch, and British colonies in the Pacific. But the U.S. was building its military might, preparing to strike back.

The Battle of Midway in June 1942 was a turning point, where the U.S. defeated the Japanese in a naval battle, destroying its main carriers. This was followed by a series of battles where the Americans slowly took back Japanese-controlled islands, such as Guam in 1944, and the victories in the Philippines and Iwo Jima in 1945. Each U.S. defeat provided the Americans with staging areas to free more islands and eventually attack Japan itself. The U.S. now had air and sea supremacy in much of the Pacific, and was moving ever closer to Japan itself.

The final major island battle was at Okinawa in April 1945. At a tremendous cost in lives to both sides, the U.S. eventually took control of the island and established airfields from which bombing attacks were launched on Japan. Despite the Japanese losses—and the fact that Germany had surrendered to the Allies on May 7, 1945—Japan still did not surrender.

At this point the U.S. was preparing for two possible options: either an invasion of Japan itself or the dropping of a weapon that had just been developed, the nuclear or atomic bomb. It was possible that both the invasion and the bomb might have to be used to conquer Japan. In preparation, most of the U.S. Navy's Pacific resources, including the USS *Indianapolis*, were being sent ever closer to Japan.

While the Japanese military was seriously weakened, they still had a number of ways to destroy the oncoming Americans, including submarines. Just where these last Japanese submarines were located was unknown, but U.S. military officials thought it likely that most would be close to the Japanese homeland to protect it from invasion. And that was one reason McVay's

Indianapolis was traveling alone. The ship was still a great many miles away—over 1,500 from the shores of Japan—where the next big battle might be fought.

~

The *Indy* had begun this mission on July 16, 1945, after undergoing extensive repairs in San Francisco. Using her massive steam turbines turning the ship's four propellers, the *Indy* traveled at an incredibly fast speed for a ship of her size of thirty-three miles per hour. After a brief stop in Pearl Harbor, she was now at Tinian, and McVay had just ordered the anchors dropped. The ship's deadly cargo, components for an atomic bomb, would be removed.

One of the men aboard the *Indy* who intently watched the off-loading of the secret cargo was Private Giles McCoy. He was part of a small detachment of marines on board the *Indy* assigned to guard the cargo, oversee the brig, and provide security for the ship.

McCoy was a mature eighteen-year-old. He was just a sophomore in high school when, while listening to his father's radio in the family's living room, he heard that the Japanese had bombed Pearl Harbor. Upon graduation he convinced his mother to sign a waiver allowing him to enter the military at age seventeen. (The standard age of induction was eighteen.)

Private McCoy felt fortunate to have been assigned to the *Indy*. On a ship, marines liked to say, no one was shooting at you, at least at close range.

But McCoy, like Captain McVay, knew danger on board a ship could come in the blink of an eye. Both had been on the *Indy* at Okinawa when a Japanese pilot steered his plane into the ship. The Japanese had found that guiding a plane directly into a ship—called a kamikaze attack, where the pilot was sure to die—was more accurate than dropping bombs. McCoy watched in alarm as the kamikaze plane zoomed down on the ship, while the *Indy*'s antiaircraft guns fired at it. But the fast-moving plane was closing in.

Captain McVay ordered the *Indy* into a hard emergency turn. For a split second it seemed the plane might miss the ship. Instead, the suicide pilot was able to both drop a five-hundred-pound bomb *and* crash his plane onto the ship's deck near the port stern.

The bomb did the greater damage, plummeting through the enlisted men's deck hall and berthing (sleeping) compartments, before exploding near the keel. Nine sailors perished. The ship was saved by damage control teams that secured watertight hatches, preventing incoming water from spreading throughout the ship.

McCoy's lasting memory of the terrible attack occurred when he and others pushed the crumpled plane off the edge of the ship before it could catch fire and explode. Staring through the cracked canopy of the plane, McCoy caught a glimpse of the dead kamikaze pilot.

Captain McVay later received a message from naval command that said: CONGRATULATIONS ON YOUR

EXCELLENT DAMAGE CONTROL. YOUR MEN DID
AN EXCELLENT JOB.

As a reward, Giles McCoy and the rest of the crew received some time off at an R&R (rest and relaxation) camp on the island of Ulithi. Here they enjoyed what they called "the three Bs": beaches, beer, and baseball.

~

Now, with the *Indianapolis* arriving at Tinian, McCoy scrutinized the wooden cargo crates about to be removed. He wondered what was in them. He knew it was something important and unusual because they had been guarded at all times. The young marine watched as the ship's crane lifted the crates and lowered them to the landing barge below. McCoy and many of the other sailors let out a cheer. They may not have known what was in the crates, but they knew this part of the mission was complete.

McCoy considered what the ship's next assignment would be. Having seen the horrors of combat up close, he grimly thought about the possible upcoming invasion of Japan. He didn't know when it would happen, but he thought he was sure to be involved.

Giles McCoy wondered if he would survive. He knew the Japanese would fight to the very last man. What he could not have known was that the enemy was close and that one of its submarines would find the young marine and his ship first.

2

INFORMATION WITHHELD

Thursday, July 26, and Friday, July 27
Tinian to Guam, and beginning of voyage toward Leyte

As the unloading of the bomb was taking place, new orders for the *Indy* had arrived. The source was the advance headquarters of the Commander in Chief, Pacific Fleet, otherwise known as CINCPAC. McVay's orders were simple: From Tinian, he was to proceed to Guam, a 120-mile cruise to the south. There he would report to the naval base for his further routing orders, or "road map," to the island of Leyte. After arriving in Leyte, he was to report by coded message to Vice Admiral Oldendorf and Rear Admiral McCormick, announcing his arrival and readiness to rejoin the Pacific Fleet. The *Indy* would also be allowed to engage in seventeen days of drills and gunnery practice.

Six hours after arriving at Tinian, the *Indy* pulled anchor, and a smiling McVay, pleased with his new plans, pointed the ship to sea, south for Guam.

As McVay sailed this night, however, the well-laid plan was already going awry. Copies of the orders directing him to report to Oldendorf and McCormick were radioed to eight different commands. However, when a member of McCormick's radio staff received the message, he decoded the name of the addressee incorrectly. Since the message appeared to be addressed not to McCormick but to another commander, the staff member stopped deciphering it altogether. He never decoded the body of the message, which described McVay's arrival. As a result, Rear Admiral McCormick did not know to expect the arrival of the USS *Indianapolis* at Leyte.

The other addressees, including Oldendorf, received the information more or less as planned. But the message didn't include the date of the *Indy*'s arrival. That would be communicated in a future dispatch.

~

En route to the island of Guam, Captain McVay was able to run his crew through antiaircraft drills, which went well. He then readied himself to report to the port director for his new routing orders. Nearing the island on July 27, the *Indy* paused at the mouth of Apra Harbor in Guam.

The *Indy* waited as a tugboat pulled back on long cables attached to an underwater net stretched across the harbor's mouth. This was meant to keep enemy subs from entering. Another tug circled behind the *Indy*, dragging in her wake sonar gear to make certain no submarines were following the ship. Once inside the harbor, the tugs pulled the net closed and the *Indy* anchored. While fuel tankers and supply ships pulled along-side the *Indy*, a motor launch arrived and McVay was ferried to shore.

Testing his land legs, McVay requested a driver and a jeep—officers never drove themselves. Soon he was being whisked along a freshly paved road that hugged the shore, past thatch huts that housed the island's few remaining natives. The road climbed above the sea, and McVay's jeep stopped atop what was called CINCPAC Hill, command center for the Pacific war theater.

Here McVay met Commodore James Carter. McVay asked if he and his ship could undertake gunnery training at Guam rather than wait for his scheduled session at Leyte. The captain was feeling the pressure of time; he wished to sharpen his crew immediately. Carter informed McVay that training was no lon-ger offered at Guam but that he could begin it at Leyte.

McVay was frustrated. At this rate, he sarcastically remarked, his men would probably receive their training off the coast of Tokyo, during the invasion. After the rather brief and unsat-isfying meeting, he joined Admiral Spruance for lunch in the officers' mess. Spruance was relaxed about the war's present state of affairs but reticent to talk details. He disclosed only that, for the moment, the invasion plans were progressing smoothly.

Essentially, there were two battle plans being waged to win the war at this time. The first involved the deployment of an estimated one million American troops to the shores of Japan. The second, the top-secret Operation Centerboard, consisted of dropping the atomic bomb, the exact outcome of which was uncertain.

After lunch, McVay was driven back down the hill to the port director's office on Apra Harbor. McVay exchanged pleasantries with one of the convoy routing officers. The two men agreed that the *Indy* should aim to arrive off Leyte on Tuesday morning, July 31. The captain was then instructed to follow what was known as the Peddie convoy route, which ran from Guam to Leyte. A journey of 1,300 miles, it had been used throughout the three and a half years of the Pacific campaign and was considered a routine transit.

McVay requested an escort for his crossing to Leyte, to protect his ship from submarines. The *Indy* had no sonar gear; detecting subs was not her job. The task of hunting enemy subs was left to destroyers, which bombed them with fifty-five-gallon drums of a highly explosive gel called Torpex. But McVay was told that an escort was not necessary. All battle-ready destroyers were already deployed in assisting the continuing B-29 raids on Japan, picking up downed pilots. They were also needed to escort transports delivering fresh troops to the forward area of Okinawa.

The *Indy* had traveled on her own before. At this point in the war, naval command assumed that she could travel safely unescorted because she was far from Japan where much of the enemy was concentrated.

McVay then asked about intelligence reports concerning enemy traffic along the route he would take to Leyte. He was told that such a report would be prepared. It would accompany his routing orders once they had been typed up. After agreeing that his navigator would retrieve both reports later that night, McVay left the office, confident that the *Indy*'s upcoming voyage would be smooth.

~

Back on the *Indy* McVay gathered the officers and told them, "We are going to Leyte to prepare for the invasion of Kyushu." The island of Kyushu was Japan's southernmost home island, located about five hundred miles from Tokyo. This was a clear indication that the *Indy* would be in the thick of the action.

McVay later received the detailed ship's orders and intelligence report, and he reviewed them with his navigator. They learned that McVay was to follow a "zigzag" course during daylight hours. At night he could use his judgment whether or not to zigzag. If visibility was good he should zigzag (an enemy sub could locate a ship better on a clear night), but if visibility was poor he had the option to sail straight ahead. Zigzagging was a defensive maneuver—the thinking being that if a moving target is hard to hit, an erratically moving target is even more elusive. In truth, the maneuver was of negligible value but was required by navy regulations.

The intelligence report seemed to contain nothing unusual. It stated that there had been three potential submarine sightings in the Peddie area where the *Indy* would be traveling. Of these, one was a report of a "sound contact" (sonar) only, and the other was a spotting of a "possible" periscope. The remaining and most credible sighting was already nearly a week old. The *Indy*'s navigator had received that information from what was called the Blue Summaries, intelligence dispatches sent out weekly by the fleet command at Pearl Harbor.

But neither the intelligence report nor the Blue Summaries included two crucial pieces of information.

Three days earlier, on July 24, the USS *Underhill*, a destroyer escort, had been sunk by a Japanese kaiten—a manned torpedo suicide craft—while sailing from Okinawa to Leyte. One hundred and twelve men had died. The kaiten had been released by a large Japanese patrol sub.

The intelligence report sent to McVay also neglected to mention another important fact. Enemy subs known as the Tamon group were known to be operating in waters around the Peddie route that the *Indy* would be following. Commodore James

Sixty feet below the Pacific's surface, in a state-of-the-art Japanese submarine, Lieutenant Commander Mochitsura Hashimoto fretted. During his four years at sea, the thirty-six-year-old submarine captain had yet to sink even one enemy ship. Now, Hashimoto knew, the war effort was verging on defeat, and he feared he might return home without a single victory. He had erected a Shinto shrine aboard the sub, and he prayed to it daily so that his luck might soon change.

Hashimoto's sub carried the latest in torpedo technology. (In this area of naval warfare, the Japanese had exceeded the American effort until the last months of the war.) The sub was in the classification of B3 types. Although the submarine did not have a name it had a number, I-58. It was 356 feet long and carried a seaplane as well as a deck-mounted machine gun for, among other things, sweeping the water clear of the torpedoed enemy's survivors.

Run by two 4,700-horsepower diesel engines, sub I-58 could cruise 21,000 miles without refueling, pushing fifteen knots on the surface. Submerged, the sub moved at seven knots. Her sausage shape was coated in a rubber girdle that distorted her echo pattern and tended to confuse American navy sonar listeners. They sometimes mistook her for a submerged whale.

On board were nineteen oxygen-powered magnetic torpedoes, and six kaitens—kamikaze-like torpedoes piloted by crewmen grateful for the honor. These sacrificial warriors would climb into the forty-eight-foot metal tubes and seat themselves in canvas chairs before a steering wheel and guidance instruments. Then the suicide sailor-pilot would wait to hear the fatal word: *Fire!*

Released from the metal bands clamping it to the sub, the kaiten began rocketing toward eternity. With a top speed of twenty knots and a range of twenty-seven miles, it was quite a sight, although it regularly missed its target as the pilot struggled to keep the speeding missile on course.

When he was successful—the kaiten was tipped with an explosive warhead—the pilot was vaporized upon impact. If the pilot missed his target, he eventually ran out of fuel, and, gliding to the ocean bottom, was fatally crushed by the immense pressure.

On the night of Saturday, July 28, the kaiten pilots were anxious for their moment of glory. But Hashimoto, peering through the periscope, scanned the night horizon of a choppy Pacific and found it blank.

For the past ten days he'd been cruising steadily south from Kure, on the Japanese mainland, without sighting a target. He had spent today on the surface in hot and squally weather, considering his next move. Stationed at the critical crossroads of the Peddie-Leyte route, he was sure a ship would pass.

~

Six hundred and fifty miles away from the Japanese sub, at 9:00 a.m. on July 28, the USS *Indianapolis* pulled away from the harbor at Guam, headed for Leyte.

The *Indy*'s doctor, Lewis Haynes, was not overly worried that the ship sailed without an escort. He had been in the thick of the war and knew his life was in danger whenever he was at sea. At age thirty-three, the doctor was one of the oldest men on board, and he and Captain McVay got along quite well.

Dr. Haynes had a wife and two young sons back in Connecticut and he was determined to make it through the war and return to them. His dedication to caring for the sick and wounded was astounding. Before being assigned to the *Indy*, he'd logged thirty-nine months without a leave (time off) while aboard destroyers and the battleship USS *New Mexico*. He never complained to his superior officers about his unusually long stint—except once, which was the same day he was awarded leave. His thinking was: He had an important job to do. And that was saving sailors' lives.

Transferred to the *Indy* in July 1944, Haynes immediately found a home where he could hone his medical skill. He had joined the navy in peacetime, in 1939, after finishing his medical schooling at Northwestern University. As a boy growing up in northern Michigan, he had watched his father practice dentistry and decided he wanted to be a surgeon.

In high school, Haynes held the state record for the 440-yard dash, and he loved to hunt grouse and fish for brook trout along the Manistee River. Michigan was wild country, and he knew it well. But when he joined the navy, he was rarely on land anymore, and to his surprise he found that he loved ship life. He especially treasured the camaraderie. Under Captain McVay, the *Indy* was more than the sum of its firepower and speed; it was a friendly town of more than 1,000 sailors. And Haynes watched over these sailors, doing whatever he could to keep them safe and healthy.

But now, unescorted by a destroyer, the *Indy* was on her own. The wisdom, concern, and protective nature of Dr. Haynes could not safeguard the ship.

TORPEDOES FIRED

Left Guam Saturday, July 28
Traveling Sunday, July 29
Torpedoes launched 12:04 a.m., July 30

The voyage was going well, and the spirits of the crew were high on the *Indy*. Down in one of the mess halls, McCoy listened to records played by the ship's onboard disc jockey, a boy from Chicago whose mother always sent him the newest records from the States. Playing lately was Benny Goodman's "Let's Dance."

Sometimes McCoy listened as Tokyo Rose, who worked for the Japanese military, butted in over the mess hall's speakers. Her mysterious voice, speaking English all the way from Japan, spooked McCoy. She often said, "We know you're out there, sailor boy. We know where you are. Don't you wish you could go home?"

On Sunday morning, July 29, the crew labored through church services in the open air of the main deck, squinting in the glare. The bitter equatorial sun soared straight up from the sea each dawn and dived into the western horizon promptly at six o'clock. The neighborly feeling among the men was strong: First to attend were the Catholics, who then relieved the Protestants from work details so they could attend their own service. Father Conway's gentle voice led the Catholic services, and his trusted friend Dr. Haynes directed the Protestant members through old hymns.

Following church services, the Sunday morning ban on smoking was lifted, and men dispersed to their various divisions to perform deck duties. After a chicken dinner—the best meal of the week, complete with strawberry shortcake—some gathered on the quarterdeck and threw around a medicine ball for exercise. Others jumped rope or sparred at boxing, refereed by Father Conway.

At some point during the early evening, after a brilliant sunset, they passed over the deepest spot on earth. The section of the Pacific Ocean they were traveling through is known as the Philippine Sea. It is an area east and northeast of the Philippines but still far from dangerous waters close to Japan. They were some three hundred miles from the nearest landfall, and a gray scrim of clouds draped the horizon.

After dark, the sailors watched a movie on the starboard hangar deck. At 9:00 p.m., "Taps" was sounded by bugle, signaling the crew (who was not on night duty) should get to their bunks.

The chief petty officer patrolled the decks looking for opened portholes leaking light into the night, and the announcement came over the PA that the "smoking lamp is now out topside." The red glow of cigarettes showed up too clearly at night; submarines could spot them.

Down in the officers' wardroom, the navigator had announced earlier that a merchant ship called *Wild Hunter* had spotted on July 28 what she thought was a periscope. A destroyer escort had been launched from Guam to investigate the report, but found nothing. The navigator also remarked that the *Indy* would be passing the spot of the sighting late in the night.

Sometime between 7:30 and 8:00 p.m., Captain McVay had given the command to cease zigzagging. His orders explicitly stated that he could do this at his discretion during times of poor visibility. The sea was running rough, with a long ground swell, and the sky was hung with low, heavy clouds, which smothered a thin strip of pale moon. At times, it was so dark that men on the bridge had to announce themselves by name.

Shortly after 10:30 p.m. McVay stepped off the bridge into the humid night air along its walkway. Belowdecks, the ship was an inferno, radiating the heat it had absorbed throughout the day. In the engine room alone, temperatures regularly exceeded 120 degrees; all hatches and doors had been opened to draw the precious salt breezes inside.

In the crew's quarters, temperatures were barely more comfortable, and many of the men chose to sleep topside, where the night air hovered in the mid-eighties. They traipsed across the deck with blanket and shoes in hand in search of relief from the humidity and heat. Some of the men crawled underneath the massive gun turrets, where they curled up against the cool steel sides of the makeshift caves. Most took off their dungarees and denim shirts and slept naked or in their underwear.

The *Indianapolis* was traveling in what was called "yoke modified" position. This was not the most secure position where all hatches and doors would be dogged—sealed off—making the compartments impermeable. "Yoke modified" described a more relaxed state of sailing. It was acceptable in waters where there was little perceived threat of enemy attack. It left the ship's interior spaces dangerously vulnerable. With the hatches opened, the otherwise watertight compartments could be breached in seconds.

At least three hundred sailors were scattered across the deck in the dark, turning restlessly, searching for sleep. McVay could hear them talking softly, or snoring, or dreaming aloud, set against the steady *shoosh* of the enormous steel bow parting the black sea. He stayed on deck for about fifteen minutes.

By 11:00 p.m., the ship was buttoned up for the night. Shortly thereafter, Captain McVay retired to his battle cabin, where he slept during times of combat vigilance. The size of a large garden shed, it was located immediately behind the chart house on the navigation bridge. If he was needed, he could be summoned either by a quick knock at his door or through what was called a "talking tube." The tube, which connected him to the bridge, pointed directly toward his ear.

The officer of the deck, in charge of the eight-to-midnight watch, was to respond to any change in their situation. If the weather and visibility improved, he was to resume zigzagging and notify the captain immediately.

In his hot, cramped cabin, McVay stripped and climbed into his bed. Beneath him, the ship hummed and throbbed, beating its way west through the murky dark, and soon he was fast asleep.

~

About twelve miles from where the USS *Indianapolis* cruised, Lieutenant Commander Hashimoto had been awakened by a subordinate officer, per orders. It was time to begin night maneuvers.

Hashimoto put on his soiled, damp uniform, laced his boots, and walked through the narrow passage of his sub. He was anxious about what the night might bring. At 11:00 p.m., he ordered the men to their night-action stations. The commander then raised the night periscope—built specifically to magnify targets in low light—and swung the serpentlike head of the instrument in a sweeping arc. Earlier, the I-58's sonarman had picked up something, which he had finally identified as the sound of rattling dishes. And this rattling was increasing, coming closer.

On the surface of the sea, the metal periscope poked through. Painted gray, it blended perfectly with the murkiness of the night and choppy sea. Yet the horizon was empty. Not a ship in sight. Hashimoto ordered the I-58 topside for a more thorough look. The boat jumped to life.

The crew blew the main ballast, releasing forced air into the tanks and jettisoning the water she had drawn upon diving three and a half hours earlier. The sub drifted silently to the surface and broke through, tons of water streaming from her gray, bulbous shape.

The crew screwed open the conning tower hatch, and the submarine's navigator climbed topside to survey the nightscape. Fresh air poured down the opening into the sub, relieving the stifling onboard conditions.

The sub's bridge was built forward on the ship, near the bow. It served as a lookout point whenever she cruised the surface. The crew stood on its metal platform, surrounded by a chest-high shield that protected them from enemy fire. The navigator scoped the horizon silently through binoculars.

Suddenly he yelled, "Bearing red, nine-zero degrees. A possible enemy ship!"

The announcement was a shock. Hashimoto had studied the same horizon but had missed the ship shrouded in darkness. The excited sub captain sprinted up the ladder onto the bridge. But he couldn't tell what he was looking at. The target was some six miles away. It was just a smudge atop the water. Hashimoto ordered the sub into a dive. The hatch was sealed, the ballast vents were opened, and the tanks began sucking in several tons of water to add weight for it to submerge. The sub slipped beneath the surface.

The hunt was on.

Down below, at his periscope, Hashimoto set about the task of working up his firing solution. This involved figuring his distance from the target, its speed, and direction. It was a tense, complicated business; each minute that elapsed gave the target more time to escape. The lieutenant commander was looking for an intercept point at which he could aim his torpedoes. As he tracked the target, he kept his eye to the periscope, determined not to lose sight of it. He had no idea if the target was also being followed by a destroyer escort.

At 11:39 p.m., six of the I-58's torpedoes were ordered loaded and ready to fire. One pilot seated himself in a kaiten, while another was ordered to stand by.

Hashimoto crept ahead at a quiet three knots.

He couldn't believe his luck.

~

Down in the sleeping compartment that contained the brig, Private McCoy was guarding two prisoners who had violated the ship's rules or a superior's orders. He had come on duty early; it had been too hot to sleep in his own compartment, where the other marines were bunked. The space was solid steel, painted gray, and it had felt like a tomb.

The narrow compartment that housed the brig and bunks for sailors wasn't much better. It was near the stern of the ship and stank of sweaty men and dirty socks, with bunks stacked four high on opposing walls. At the forward end stood a ladder that led topside, the only way in and out of the compartment. To the left of the ladder were the two jail cells.

McCoy watched the sailors he was supposed to keep an eye on turn restlessly in their bunks. He felt sorry for the two sailors he'd guarded since the ship's departure from San Francisco. They were serving a two-week sentence, ostensibly living on a diet of bread and water. But their buddies from the kitchen were always bringing them sandwiches and pie. McCoy generally looked the other way.

Swish ping, swish ping, came the relentless pounding of the sea against the hull. McCoy hoped to hell he'd make it out of this war alive. He had another two years in his hitch to go. Around his neck he wore a string of rosary beads given to him by his mom.

He shone the light on the jailed sailors, checking to make sure they were asleep. Then McCoy settled in, looking forward to getting off duty at 4:00 a.m.

~

In the forward part of the ship, Dr. Lewis Haynes stood in a doorway to the wardroom, watching a lively game of bridge. Haynes was exhausted. He'd given 1,000 cholera inoculations to the crew that day in preparation for the coming invasion. There was no telling what diseases the wounded prisoners coming off the beach might bring to the ship.

Haynes knew some of the sailors were nervous about the future. They talked to him about lots of things. Mostly, they chatted about problems at home with girlfriends or fiancées. A sailor could be wrecked by a "green banana," a letter from his sweetheart telling him she was seeing another guy. And aboard ship, there was no way to get rid of the hurt. Or the longing.

One of the card players looked up to ask if Haynes wanted to be dealt in. Haynes thought a moment, then responded: "Naw, you men go ahead. I'm a damn lousy card player." Then he turned away and continued down the passageway to his cabin.

Haynes drew the curtain to his berth, stripped, and pulled on white cotton pajama pants. Tomorrow would be a busy day. He would be up at reveille to inspect the mess halls and the crew's living quarters with the captain. Then he'd attend to the sick crew, half of whom weren't really sick; they only wanted to be excused from deck duty. When Haynes found a sailor who was faking illness, he'd bark, "Don't give me that shit!" and send him back to work. Still, he couldn't help but smile at the ingenuity of some of the men's imagined stomachaches and muscle sprains.

Then, his day finally done, he slid beneath the sheets and fell asleep almost instantly.

~

Ensign Harlan Twible, twenty-three, just two weeks out of the Naval Academy, stood in the elevated metal crow's nest eighty feet off the main deck, watching the night sky. Heavy clouds scudded across the moon. It was what the sailors called a "peeka-boo night"; right now Twible couldn't see his hand in front of his face.

Twible was standing watch with Leland Clinton. The two had gotten friendly during the past two weeks. Clinton was a farmer's son from the Midwest; Twible's parents were Irish mill workers from Massachusetts. Getting into the academy had been a dream come true for Twible. As an ensign, he was at the bottom of the officer ratings, but he was determined to work his way up.

Using a telephone, he could communicate with the bridge. If he spotted a plane or torpedo, he could quickly ring the news through, and the general alarm for battle stations would be called. But now he saw nothing but a rough sea, with long, deep swells rolling across the ocean from the northeast. Since July 27, a typhoon had been moving southwest from Okinawa, and it was gathering strength.

About twenty men were stationed around the ship in simi-lar positions of vigilance, each overlooking a separate quadrant of the ship's horizon. There were four officers on duty on the bridge. The officer of the deck, Lieutenant John Orr, was in charge of communication with Captain McVay if any changes were needed in the ship's maneuvers.

The supervisor of the night's watch, thirty-seven-year-old

Lieutenant Commander K. C. Moore, was charged with keeping an overall eye on both Orr and the operation of the bridge and engine rooms. Moore checked the night watches and lookouts about the ship and found all of them alert.

~

Three miles away and closing in on the *Indy*, Lieutenant Commander Hashimoto studied the blurred outline of the ship through the periscope. Hashimoto racked his brain trying to accurately identify the vessel. It was crucial. Lying open on a table near the periscope was a book of U.S. warship silhouettes that provided intelligence necessary to correctly identify battleships, carriers, and cruisers. The book also presented important information about each ship's speed and capabilities.

Hashimoto knew the ship wasn't friendly, because he'd been kept apprised of Japanese naval movement through coded dispatches. It had to be enemy, but what kind? He studied the approaching shape through the periscope. Destroyer? Battleship? Why was it headed straight at him? He wondered if it was a destroyer hunting him.

He ordered his sub on a new course heading to port, or to his left. Through the periscope, the bridge and superstructure of the ship became more clearly visible as a triangle shape. Now the ID could be made. Hashimoto incorrectly surmised that this target was of the battleship class. He announced this as the sub's sonarman tuned in to the sound of the approaching ship's engine revolutions. Hashimoto counted the revolutions for one minute, calculating the target's speed.

It was twenty knots. The commander next swung his sub into position to meet the *Indy* broadside for the kill shot. From this vantage, he could see that his target, illuminated by the sliver of moon peeking through the clouds, was indeed a large ship.

As the attack procedure progressed, the four kaiten pilots became more and more adamant that one of them be launched. But in the excitement of the sudden rush to identify the ship, Hashimoto had actually forgotten about them. He now told the pilots that because of the conditions, with the target closing in, it would be nearly impossible to miss the kill; their lives would be wasted unnecessarily if he used them.

Then, with his eye pressed to the rubber cup of the periscope, Hashimoto gave the order to fire. It was 12:04 a.m.

The first torpedo shot from a forward tube of the sub and quickly accelerated to a cruising speed of forty-eight knots, or about as fast as a racing greyhound. It traveled at a depth of thirteen feet, leaving behind a swirling wake.

The torpedo carried 1,210 pounds of explosives. Hashimoto fired six of these, and they left the sub at three-second intervals, in a widening fan of white lines.

Hashimoto was certain one or more of the torpedoes would hit the ship and send it to the bottom of the sea.

PART II

FIRES SPREADING

*On board the ship when the torpedoes
hit and moments after, July 30*

It took less than a minute for two of the torpedoes to intercept the *Indianapolis*.

At 12:05 a.m. all hell broke loose.

The first torpedo hit the forward starboard, or right side, and tore part of the bow away. Men were thrown fifteen feet in the air. Those who weren't blown in two landed on their feet, stunned, their ears ringing.

The second explosion occurred closer to midship and was even more massive.

Carter, with whom McVay had met at CINCPAC headquarters, knew about the *Underhill* sinking and the Tamon submarines, but he did not mention either to McVay. Carter assumed that McVay would be apprised of the situation when he received his routing orders from a Lieutenant Waldron, the convoy and routing officer.

Captain McVay, however, was not apprised of the situation. This was because the existence of the Tamon submarines had been deduced by ULTRA, an extremely top-secret code-breaking program.

ULTRA had been used during the Battle of Midway to pinpoint and annihilate Japanese naval forces. Several days after the battle, however, U.S. newspapers reported that American forces had learned the positions of the Japanese ships and troops, and the effect in turn was disastrous. Within the week, the Japanese changed their encrypting system, stumping the U.S. The ULTRA program had to waste precious time to re-crack the new Japanese system of encryption.

U.S. military command determined that the secrecy of ULTRA would thereafter be maintained at all costs. This included the decision to avoid sinking certain enemy ships when the navy knew their precise whereabouts. The hope was to lull the Japanese navy into a sense of security. As a result of these security measures, McVay was left in the dark about what lay ahead of him down the Peddie route.

~

The sea itself seemed to be burning. The first torpedo had smashed one gas tank containing 3,500 gallons of high-octane aviation fuel, igniting a burning river that reduced the bulkheads and doors to red-hot slabs of steel. The fuel incinerated everything in its path.

The second torpedo had pierced the four-inch steel armor below the bridge. Also hit were the *Indy*'s boiler rooms, which provided steam to the ship's forward engine room, called engine room 1. Both torpedoes had smashed into the starboard side of the ship, actually lifting the ship off the water. The *Indianapolis* paused like a large beast struck between the ribs, then settled back in the water, plowing ahead at seventeen knots. With her bow damaged, she began scooping up seawater by the ton.

It was 12:06 a.m.—just a minute after the torpedoing. The ship had been cut nearly in half. All compartments and crew forward of the number-one smokestack were struggling for life. Those areas aft of the stack, including radio shack 2 and engine room 2, as well as compartments belowdecks such as the post office and the mess halls, initially were relatively untouched by the explosions. Within minutes, though, this situation changed. Soon the armory, library, log room, and marine compartment were in flames, the mess halls choked with smoke and dust.

The ship began to slightly list, or tilt, to her starboard side. She had only minutes left afloat, and those aboard her had seconds to decide their fate.

Chief Engineer Richard Redmayne had been in the officers' head, standing at the toilet, when the explosion shook the compartment. The torpedo hit less than thirty feet away. Redmayne smelled smoke and heard flames licking the starboard passageway on the other side of the door. Steeling himself, he ran out.

Badly burned, Redmayne dashed through fallen debris and billowing smoke to engine room 2, about three hundred feet from the bow. There he found everything in working order.

All the generators around him were operating and supplying power. From midship back, the ship generally had power and lights, supplied by the auxiliary diesel generators. Redmayne tried to use the telegraph and found it dead. He wanted desperately to contact the bridge for a report and further orders. But that was impossible.

Stunned and terrified, Redmayne didn't have the slightest idea of the bedlam in engine room 1. He wasn't even sure what had caused the explosions. Reading his gauges, he discovered that the power was dropping in the engine that controlled one of the propellers. Redmayne believed the ship mustn't stop if she'd been torpedoed. Since he couldn't consult with Captain McVay or the damage control officer, he had to make a judgment call. He ordered the remaining propeller to turn faster.

~

Up in his battle cabin, Captain McVay had been lifted straight off his bed and slammed to the floor. Rising, he stumbled through clouds of white smoke, his throat scorched from the acrid odor of the burning ship. Immediately, he kicked into battle mode and began collecting himself within a whirlwind of conflicting thoughts. Had they been hit by a kamikaze? Run into a floating mine? Were they under attack? The ship's vibrations reminded the experienced captain of the kamikaze attack off Okinawa.

McVay quickly ruled out mines because he remembered they were too far out to sea for the Japanese to have strewn the water with the deadly floating spheres. He thought he detected a whipping sensation, as if the ship were shaking from side to side. He reasoned that the shaking of the deck and bulkheads was too violent for a single kamikaze plane to have caused.

The only rational explanation was that they'd been torpedoed. McVay had never encountered this precise kind of disaster before, but he knew his duties. He had three pressing jobs: Assess the damage, take care of it, and engage the enemy—if indeed they were in battle.

Most dreaded of all was the possibility that the captain would have to give the call to abandon ship if the damage was beyond control. But for now, his first concern was to get off distress messages detailing the ship's condition and position. He stumbled nude and barefoot from his cabin to the bridge.

When McVay walked onto the twenty-foot-wide bridge platform, he found it in chaos. The darkness was so thick that the men had to identify themselves by name. McVay knew he needed to establish order by determining the extent of the damage. He looked for his damage control officer, K. C. Moore, but couldn't find him.

What McVay didn't know was that the water mains used for fighting fire had been ruined. Damage control efforts had proved impotent against the spreading inferno. Crews lugged heavy hoses across what remained of the forward deck and screwed them into hydrants, only to throw the valves open and find they had no water pressure.

Other crew members, under Moore's direction, were operating a series of valves spaced throughout the ship that opened and closed certain compartments. These could be filled and emptied with seawater in an attempt to balance the ship's list. So far, the measures, along with the dogging of the hatches of the blown area, were failing to halt the flooding or slow the increasing list of the *Indianapolis*.

On the bridge, McVay turned to the matter of getting off a distress signal. He ordered Commander Johns Janney belowdecks to radio shack 1. It was imperative that their latitude and longitude positions be broadcast repeatedly.

"Get the message out that we've been torpedoed," the captain told his trusted navigator, "and that we need assistance, on the double!"

Janney raced from the bridge. McVay would never see him again.

The captain next yelled for his officer of the deck, Lieutenant Orr. The young officer ran to the captain and snapped to attention at his side. The twenty-two-year-old Annapolis graduate was deeply upset, knowing that as the *Indy* continued sailing, she was rapidly taking on water.

Orr calmed himself enough to explain that because the electrical system was out, he couldn't talk with the engine room. "I have tried to stop the engines," he told McVay. "I don't know whether the order has ever gotten through."

McVay took the news in; this was the first report he'd heard of the ship's condition, and he was still undecided about its severity. Judging from the slight list and the probability that the back half of the ship hadn't suffered any damage at all, it seemed likely that the *Indy* could be saved.

McVay rushed back to his battle cabin. He grabbed his clothes, and returned to his command post, dressing as he awaited Janney. But Janney did not return and the captain didn't know if the emergency radio message had gone out.

Shortly, Quartermaster Bob Gause entered the dark, smoke-filled bridge.

McVay asked Gause if he had any idea what had happened to Commander Janney.

"Captain," Gause said, "there is no radio shack 1. It's all blown to hell."

McVay was surprised. The situation was sounding more disastrous by the minute.

~

The ship was crawling with stunned sailors. All awaited the next order. A majority of the men were still under the impression that this was an air battle. They thought maybe they'd been hit by a

Betty—a Japanese plane that released armor-piercing bombs. Or maybe they'd been shelled by an enemy battleship. Who knew?

With one propeller still turning, the *Indy* was plowing ahead now at about twelve knots, or fourteen miles per hour, and the list was increasing by the minute. With her bow torn off, the front of the ship resembled a mangled snout rooting ahead through the sea, gulping water. The massive incoming water was punching through auxiliary bulkheads, taking on a life of its own. It roared back through the ship toward the stern, seeking out all dry places.

Damage Control Officer K. C. Moore had been running through the ship, trying to secure the most badly breached compartments. The key was to stop the flooding before it pulled the ship underwater, but the damage control officer was having trouble finding any repair parties to aid him.

Even if Moore had found help, it would be of little use. The second torpedo had torn open a gaping hole forty feet in diameter in the side of the ship. Thousands of gallons of fuel oil were pouring out, trailing the ship like a liquid scarf. Desks, mattresses, books, papers, clothing, bodies, and pieces of bodies were sucked out through the hole as the contents of the ship were exchanged for the incoming breach of the sea.

Already roughly one hundred men were dead—burned, blown up, or drowned. Most of those sleeping forward of the 8-inch guns on the bow had been vaporized. The bodies that remained were charred beyond recognition.

As the water poured into the ship, the sailors who had

managed to survive the explosions tried climbing up ladders to the deck. They found themselves turned back by fires raging above them. Others, racing through the narrow passageways toward the dogged hatches of the stern, were trapped by the accumulating water. All the while the ship continued its starboard lean.

Topside, those sailors forward of the bridge, nearest the bow, saw that the deck was mangled. They also noticed that the steel plating was split in places and that smoke and flames were pouring from these fissures. Men standing or lying on the deck in various stages of pain and disbelief were being seared on the superheated steel. The night was filled with screams and explosions that faded over the water.

The *Indy* was alone, cut off, struggling to stay afloat.

~

McVay was still anxiously awaiting a report from radio shack 1. His hope was that if radio central was blown, emergency radio 2 could broadcast their location. McVay's thoughts were interrupted by K. C. Moore, who burst onto the bridge. Out of breath, the damage control officer informed the captain that the ship's forward compartments were flooding quickly. "We're badly damaged, sir," he announced. "Do you want to call for abandon ship?"

It was now around 12:11 a.m. and the ship had slowed to about nine knots, or ten miles per hour. Since the explosions, her forward momentum and her remaining power had managed to push her about one mile across the ocean.

McVay had little time to react. He simply couldn't believe that the damage could be so severe, given the short time frame. It defied reason and his experience when the ship was earlier attacked at Okinawa and stayed afloat. He knew he had to be certain the *Indy* was sinking before he ordered abandon ship.

"Maybe we can hold her," he told Moore. "Go below and take one more look and report back to me immediately."

Moore hurried belowdecks to check the situation again. It was the last McVay would see of him.

Almost immediately Commander Joseph Flynn, the ship's second in command, arrived and briefed McVay on the *Indy*'s worsening situation. The ship was now listing at a perilous angle.

Below McVay and Flynn, the wounded sailors who were strong enough tried to compensate for the deck's list by walking hand over hand along the ship's lifelines. Those too badly injured stumbled and crashed into bulkheads. Or kept rolling, cartwheeling into the sea.

Flynn told McVay that the *Indy* was flooding fast. Then came the final blow: "We are definitely going down. I suggest that we abandon ship."

McVay was stunned. However, he trusted Flynn's report. Combined with his damage control officer's earlier assessment, it convinced McVay that there was nothing else to be done.

"Pass the word to abandon ship," he announced.

Just eight minutes had passed since the torpedoes struck.

5

ABANDON SHIP!

Moments after the torpedoing, July 30

The *Indy* was indeed going down.

The ship was slowing, but not quickly enough, and she was still taking on water. With the bow gone, the remaining forward part of the ship, about 150 feet, was weakening, threatening to blow off under the force of the water rushing against it. Besides the list to the starboard side, the bow rode much lower in the water than the stern.

The ship rumbled and groaned as it punched through the heavy, fifteen-foot swells. Belowdecks, the men heard roars like thunder as machinery and equipment smashed into bulkheads, and other compartments were breached by the powerful sea.

Normally, the announcement McVay was about to make would come over the ship's PA (public address speakers), but the PA was gone, along with electricity to the power lines. Moving quickly to the bridge's port side, he cupped his hands to his mouth and yelled down to the several hundred sailors gathered at the rail below, "Abandon ship!"

Now they began jumping off one by one, then they began to go in droves, jumping in a wave that swept toward the stern of the ship. Although almost all had life preservers, some were too terrified to jump and stood frozen—they were pushed from behind and dropped out of sight into the sea.

Like a crowd trying to rush a gate, some four hundred crew members crowded the rail at the port stern. A young lieutenant who hadn't heard the order to abandon ship had been trying to hold the sailors at bay, screaming, "Don't jump yet!"

The lieutenant soon gave up and was nearly crushed as the men struggled to climb onto the rail and steady themselves. They stepped off into space and plummeted close to eighty feet, screaming as they dropped into the dark sea below.

In the chaos and confusion—exacerbated by the loss of the PA system—approved procedures for leaving the *Indy* were forgotten or at best carried out in haphazard fashion. All of this was compounded by the fact that during the ship's high-speed run to Tinian, the green hands on board hadn't had much time to practice any of the abandon ship procedures.

In the theoretical process, life rafts and motor launches are dropped into the water. Then rope ladders and nets are lowered over the side of the ship, providing access to the life rafts, which are stowed with various lifesaving provisions. Survival gear in 1945 included mess utensils; first aid kits; flare guns, signal flags, reflecting mirrors, rifles, and ammunition.

On the *Indy*, the two motor-launch whaleboats, stationed near the stern—each twenty-six feet long and intended to carry twenty-two men—had been undamaged by the torpedoing. Nearby, stacked like giant pieces of gray bread, were about seven of the thirty-five cork and canvas-covered rafts. Each raft was able to hold twenty-five men. (These were distributed in equal numbers around the ship, but those at the bow had been rendered useless.)

Each craft was supposed to be outfitted with bread sealed in watertight cans and potable water in wooden beakers, or kegs. The whaleboats were meant to be equipped with a boat chest containing a hatchet, a hammer, a screwdriver, pliers, sailmaker's needles, lamp wicks, sail twine, a seven-inch fishing reel with line and assorted hooks and sinkers, lanterns, oil, and matches.

Of the thirty-five life rafts stacked on board, about twelve made it off the ship, and these carried few of the specified provisions. In the hubbub of the *Indy*'s quick departure from San Francisco, some of the water kegs apparently had not been filled. In many of those that had not been recently replenished, the existing water had turned foul in the wooden containers. Few boat chests had been loaded into the life rafts.

On the other hand, luck had been with the men of the *Indy*

because there were more life vests than sailors. Twenty-five hundred life vests—along with a large number of life belts—were stored throughout the ship. As the *Indy* tilted beneath their feet, the sailors clamored to reach them.

~

Captain McVay worried that the distress messages from radio shacks 1 and 2 hadn't gotten off. The crew's survival depended on getting help as quickly as possible. In a little less than thirty-six hours, when the ship didn't arrive in Leyte, McVay assumed she would be reported missing. But the captain was concerned that many of the injured would not be able to survive the wait. He walked from the bridge to the ladder leading to the main deck and started down. He wanted to see for himself, up close, what had happened to his ship.

Just as McVay reached the communications deck, the ship violently wrenched to sixty degrees. Below him, on the starboard side, he spied sailors preparing to jump overboard without life jackets.

"No, men!" he yelled. "Don't go over unless you have one of these!" He pointed frantically at his own jacket. It was too late—the men were leaping anyway. Nearby, seaman Jack Cassidy, an eighteen-year-old from West Springfield, Massachusetts, looked up from the deck where he knelt. He saw McVay silhouetted by flames erupting from the bow. Their eyes locked for a moment. McVay cried out, "God bless you!"

Within seconds, the *Indy* rolled to ninety degrees. The ship was now lying on her right side.

McVay jumped to the forecastle deck and crawled up to the rail. He did some quick calculations in his head—it was clear the radio shack was unreachable and, in fact, was in imminent danger of flooding. The back portion of the ship, from the bridge to the stern, was crawling with men. McVay started heading aft.

The sailors still inside the ship—an estimated one hundred or so—found themselves walking on the bulkheads or crushed by loose machinery and equipment set flying. The deck had suddenly disappeared from beneath them. Men trapped on the lower starboard rail tried desperately to climb the deck to the higher port side. They lifted themselves hand over hand using railings, ladders, and stray lines, much like men scaling a sheer cliff face.

~

ORDEAL OF CASSIDY, McCOY

Seaman Jack Cassidy was hacking frantically at the plaster cast on his leg with a knife. He'd wrenched it in gunnery practice during the journey from Pearl Harbor. With a final slice, the cast slid off, and he climbed up the deck to the high port side. Standing on the rail, Cassidy looked forward to the bow and saw dead bodies strewn about the bent metal plates. He leaped, flinging himself as far from the ship as he was able. Naked except for a thin pair of worn dungaree shorts, Cassidy clutched a rubber life belt that he hadn't had time to blow up. He hit the water and began swimming. Then curiosity got the better of him; he turned and saw the ship flaring with explosions that moved through the forward sections in an eerie strobe effect.

Back on board, men with knives slashed at bags of life jackets and floater nets. Trying to free one of the *Indy*'s twenty-six-foot whaleboats, a sailor was crushed as the deck slid beneath him and he found himself pinned to the ship's bulkhead under the heavy wooden craft.

At this point, about eleven minutes had passed since the torpedoes struck. The men leaving on the high, port side were sliding down the long expanse of exposed hull, which was mercifully clear of barnacles as a result of the *Indy*'s overhaul in San Francisco. They entered the water with a splash, screaming as they dropped.

On the low side of the ship, the starboard rail was now level with the water itself. Sailors on this side could walk off like swimmers stepping into a pool. Some stepped off without even getting their hair wet. They settled with the lightest of splashes and began swimming away.

It was here, depending on which side of the ship they left, that the crew began to seal different fates for themselves. Those who departed from the port side entered a sea nearly devoid of any lifesaving equipment. Because the ship was heeling to the right, or starboard, all the lifesaving gear was sliding down the deck and into the sea in that direction.

The men leaving the *Indy* from the lower starboard rail bobbed along with empty powder cans, wooden desks and chairs, papers, and crates of potatoes and carrots. Loose life vests and rafts were also floating in the water off this low side. The men needed to work fast, collecting what they could before swimming as far as possible away from the ship, whose burning hulk was now threatening to roll over on top of them.

Regardless of which side of the ship they exited, the sailors were swimming directly into the poisonous field of black fuel oil spewing from the ship's exploded hull. It was sticky as molasses, and they couldn't avoid swallowing it as they paddled around in the heavy swells. It smothered them in a noxious blanket, clogging their eyes, ears, and mouths.

Many simply drifted in shock. All that was visible of their blackened faces was the whites of their eyes and their red, screaming mouths.

Chaos was at full fiery whirl.

~

McCoy knew something very bad had happened. However, there was no smoke, fire, or loss of electricity in the brig. It was hard for him to figure out what exactly was going on. He was completely unaware of the terror unfolding in the forward area of the ship. Before the hit, McCoy, dressed in a green T-shirt and fatigues, had been standing beneath an air vent. Then: *Wham!*

The lights had blacked out, and the compartment rang like a

gong. McCoy had been tossed fifteen feet across the brig to an opposite wall, where he hit a bunk. This set into motion a chain reaction of bunks falling to the floor. McCoy stood up and felt for broken bones. He was fine.

McCoy's first thought was that the *Indy* had been rammed by a Japanese destroyer. Or that maybe the ship had hit a mine. He had no idea. One thing he *was* sure of: His first order of duty was to help the wounded out of the sleeping compartment adjoining the brig, then hurry to his battle station at the 5-inch gun located aft on the ship. All around him, sailors were screaming out in pain. McCoy searched around the pitch-dark interior, found a big nine-volt-cell battle light, and shone it over the gray metal walls of the compartment.

About thirty enlisted men had been thrown from their bunks into a tangle on the deck. In the pale beam of his light, McCoy could see the fall had knocked a few of them out. He knelt and felt for pulses, and tried shaking them back to consciousness. It was no good—they were either dead or unconscious.

McCoy worried about the closing of the hatches. He didn't want to be in this compartment if an order was given to shut them. He knew he had to move fast.

Behind him, the two prisoners yelled to be let out of their cells, and McCoy quickly fumbled for the key and released them. All three turned their attention to the wounded. Some had broken legs, arms, and ribs. About twenty of the thirty men were now stirring, writhing, and begging McCoy to move the bunks off them.

McCoy and the two sailors from the jail, breathing heavily in the foul heat, began untangling their crewmen. Then they escorted them up the steep, metal ladder through the hatch—the only way out. It was hard work, and they were frantic to keep moving as quickly as possible. About eight minutes after the explosion, a chief petty officer appeared in the black square of night filling the open hatch. McCoy could see he was agitated.

"We're gonna have to dog this hatch, Private!"

"But there's men still down here!"

"Well, get 'em out!"

This was what every sailor feared: that the men who couldn't be moved would be entombed forever within the ship.

They upped their pace, but by the time the chief petty officer reappeared McCoy guessed that there were nine men still in the compartment. The sailors from the brig dashed up the ladder and disappeared into the night. Looking up the rungs leading to the hatch, McCoy could see the night sky pinned with clouds. He couldn't bear the thought of leaving the compartment. Sensing that their fate was being settled, the sailors left behind cried: "Don't leave us. Don't leave us."

McCoy barked, "I'm coming!" at the chief petty officer. Next, with a sick feeling of anguish over leaving men behind, he ran up the ladder without looking back. There was nothing he could do. A few seconds later, he heard the clang of the hatch closing. Then came the rasp of the pin as it was inserted into the locked position.

The men trapped inside were screaming, but the sound was

tinny and faint. McCoy knew the horrors of the night were just beginning.

Reaching the main deck, he steadied himself on the high port rail, then he started toward the bow. He saw men scrambling across the pitched deck, faces burned and blackened, wailing. They seemed out of their minds.

McCoy could hear the ship hiss as it slowly settled lower in the water. Looking down, he realized he was wearing only one shoe—he was holding the other. He quickly jammed it on his foot and inched along the rail, found a life vest, and snatched it up without stopping. He felt the ship shaking beneath him as explosions sounded throughout her interior. It was like riding a thunderhead. Ahead, he could see that the bow was completely underwater. The ship's rails were driving through the sea. It was then that he realized that the *Indy* was really going to sink.

The deck gave one final turn. Slipping, McCoy grabbed the loose ends of some wiring, wrapped it around his fists, and began climbing up a tilted gun mount.

He pulled himself over the splinter shield, a large square plate of steel that protected the gunners, and stood on top of it. *It's now or never,* he thought.

McCoy stepped off onto the side of the ship and began walking down the metal hull, converging with a swarm of about thirty sailors, all headed for the sea. He dropped into a crouch, sat down, lifted his feet, and slid across the keel. With a splash, the young marine hit the water and was smothered in the blanket of leaking fuel oil.

McCoy surfaced, gagging. He shook his head, then tried wiping his eyes, but this only smeared more oil into them. And then he began to swim. Looking over his shoulder, he could see one of the ship's inboard propellers still spinning. Men were jumping off the stern, screaming as they dropped. They hit the blades and were thrown into the air. One minute they were dropping straight for the sea; the next, they were flying sideways, wailing as they flew out into the darkness.

6

RADIO MESSAGES IGNORED

Moments after torpedoing, July 30

ORDEAL OF DR. HAYNES

Asleep in his private berth in the forward part of the ship, Dr. Lewis Haynes had been knocked high into the air when the first torpedo hit. He'd just managed to stand up on wobbly legs when the second explosion knocked him down again.

Haynes grabbed his life jacket from its hook by the door. Then he took one last look at the framed picture of his wife and hurried through the curtain into the passageway, where he was greeted by the sound of tortured screaming.

The doctor paused to try to locate the source: It was Lieutenant

Commander Henry, the dentist, next door. Haynes was paralyzed by the sounds of mortal agony; it was clear that the man was burning up in his room. With the dentist's screams still in his ears, he pushed on down the passage.

There he met Lieutenant Commander Ken Stout, who emerged from smoke gathering in thick plumes along the ceiling of the hall. "Look out, Lew!" Stout yelled, and Haynes lifted his hands to his face. A tremendous burst of a flash fire—*fwoom!*—scoured the hall. Haynes heard the snap and fizzle of wires shorting out. Farther away, near the bow, there were more explosions. For a moment, Haynes believed he was on fire himself, so intense was the heat and pain.

The fire had, in fact, singed Haynes's hair, forehead, and hands, giving him what he knew from experience were third-degree burns. When he was able to open his eyes, Stout had disappeared. All that remained was the harsh scent of burned skin.

Stepping through the smoke, the doctor headed toward the officers' wardroom. He was trying to reach the quarterdeck, his battle station, anxious to get to work and do what he could for the injured. Stumbling into the wardroom, he was overcome by the noxious smoke of the gray paint burning off the bulkheads. The room was filled with a red haze. In one corner, a man was trying to beat out a fire burning in a pile of rags on the floor. Barely able to see, Haynes felt his way along the hot bulkheads with his burned hands, trying to find a way out toward the stern. Then he tripped over a chair, grabbed at the air, and collapsed into a sitting position.

He looked around the room. He was dying now, and he knew it. In spite of his fear, he had no desire to move farther, to safety. He slumped over, feeling nothing.

Looming above him suddenly was a person. It was another officer, equally dazed, who screamed, "My God, I'm fainting," then tripped over the chair that had waylaid Haynes. The officer—Haynes couldn't identify him—fell across his legs and came to rest in his lap.

Instantly Haynes stood up, as if waking from a bad dream. He had no idea where he was. The unconscious officer tumbled to the floor, and Haynes stepped over him, hearing a voice in a corner of the room calling out, "Open a porthole!"

A porthole? Yes! That might be a good idea. The notion wormed its way into the doctor's consciousness as he lurched across the room. Finding one open, Haynes jammed his head through. The relief was instant; he drew in the humid night air with deep, invigorating breaths. Then, looking down, he saw the gaping hole in the ship's side, and a steady stream of debris exiting it.

Something wet slapped him in the face. It was a rope. It occurred to him that he might be able to wiggle out the porthole and climb the line up the side of the ship to safety. It was not an easy move, especially given his burns. But it was the only way out. He would have to try.

The doctor grabbed the rim of the porthole. First he stuck his right arm and shoulder through and kicked with his feet, like a man swimming in air. This eased him through the opening enough so that he could then squeeze his left arm through.

Carefully, he twisted around so that he was lying on his back in the porthole, then moved himself into a seated position.

He gripped the line. The pain in his hands was excruciating. Looking up, he could see a climb of about five feet to the deck above. He gritted his teeth and began pulling, raising hand over hand. As he neared the top, the screaming from the quarterdeck grew louder. He hoisted himself to the lifelines and stepped through them.

The scene was horrifying: Spread before him were several dozen wounded men in various stages of delirium, some burned beyond recognition. Several were walking about in a daze, clothes scorched from their bodies, hair smoking.

Do something—do anything, Haynes thought. But what? These men needed a hospital—many of them, he saw, would shortly die from their wounds. During abandon ship drills, the wounded had been instructed to gather on the quarterdeck. Here Haynes saw that his pharmacist's mate, John Schmueck, had pulled some cots from one of the hangars and was lifting those who could be moved onto them. He'd also found a first aid box. When Haynes joined him, Schmueck handed over a stethoscope and a packet of morphine Syrettes (hollow needles, syringes, filled with the painkiller morphine). The sailors were in such bad shape that Haynes quickly began shooting them up with the drug without asking questions or performing even cursory examinations.

When he started to run out of morphine and then gauze bandages, he ordered a sailor to retrieve some supplies from the sick bay. The sailor ran to the ladder at the end of the quarterdeck, took one look down, and sprinted back to Haynes. "There ain't no sick bay," he shouted.

Water was rising up the passage. An officer rushed up to Haynes's side. "You better get some life vests on these men, Doc!" he screamed through the smoke.

Dropping their syringes and rolls of bandages, Haynes and Schmueck ran across the deck and up a ladder to the next deck. Here, men were cutting down life vests and passing them out to a constant flow of men. Haynes grabbed as many as he could, and then he and Schmueck ran back down the ladder to their writhing patients.

Haynes approached a burned man. As he loosely tied the canvas straps around the man, he kept telling him, "I have to do this. I have to do this." The man screamed as Haynes pulled the vest snug. And then Haynes turned his attention to the next wounded man. Working steadily by the weak light of an intermittent moon, he tried his best as his heart broke.

What happened next was almost too much to bear, but he watched without averting his eyes. The hangar was by now filled with cots containing patients, and as the ship lurched to starboard, these men began sliding down the deck—first one at a time, then in groups. Gaining speed, they crashed into the water. Haynes watched as one man wearing a leg cast clawed at the air and then sank without a sound.

The helpless doctor crawled up the quarterdeck, which by now was listing at about sixty degrees, and grabbed at the lifelines. Nearby, about twenty steps away, a life raft and floater net were fastened to the bulkhead. The latter, made of heavy twine, was edged with thick cork floats. The weight of the net and the raft bore down toward the starboard rail. He could lift neither.

There was nothing left to do but leave the ship.

Dr. Haynes started slowly walking down the gray hull, amid a frightened crowd of men. After about fifteen steps, Haynes reached the bulbous keel. Here and there, little bouquets of flame twisted on the water.

And then Haynes jumped.

Quickly, he began stroking away. When he turned to look back, the stern of the ship was pointing almost straight up at the sky. He saw men standing motionless on one of the giant, stilled propellers on the port side. They looked like figurines perched atop a beastly flower made of brass—riding the ship into the sea.

~

As the *Indy* sank, a radioman in radio shack 1 sent out distress signals giving her longitude and latitude positions. WE HAVE BEEN HIT BY TORPEDOES. NEED IMMEDIATE ASSISTANCE. It seemed doubtful that there was power enough to successfully transmit these pleas for help. In fact, the radioman was working with a dead key. Radio shack 1, normally used to send messages, bore the brunt of the second torpedo. The cables connecting the transmitters to the transmitting keys had been severed.

Radio shack 2, located several hundred feet away, near

the stern, had remained up and running after the hit. Radio Technician Jack Miner, fresh from Yale University, had only been aboard the *Indy* two weeks. Miner entered radio shack 2 shortly after the torpedoing. There he found his superior officer, Chief Radio Electrician L. T. Woods, trying to improvise sending a signal on equipment that wasn't normally meant for the job.

Woods grabbed Miner by the shoulders and positioned him squarely in front of one of the transmitters. Woods ordered Miner to warm up this transmitter, then went to work on one nearby, which operated on another frequency.

Once Miner had warmed up his equipment, he watched as Woods found a solution to the problem. Sticking out from the front of Woods's transmitter was a toggle resembling a light switch. Woods knew that if he flipped it up and down, he could send a series of signals—on-off, on-off—similar to the keying of the telegraph pad. Because the switch didn't automatically spring back once it had been pressed down, Woods had to flip it in a staccato series of clicks.

Miner was amazed by Woods's calmness. He watched the red, hair-thin needle in the meter monitor jump with each flip of the toggle switch. This meant that power was circling through the transmitter and traveling from the cables to the antennae. Woods keyed for about two minutes, clicking out the SOS and the ship's coordinates.

The two were so intent on the work that they completely lost track of the ship's increasingly starboard list. When Miner broke himself away from the red-needle trance, he realized that the radio shack was heeled on its side at a steep angle. He and Woods kept falling downward into the machinery. Woods finally yelled, "Okay, abandon ship!"

Miner stepped out of the room and went tumbling down the deck and into the sea.

Suddenly he was surrounded by darkness, as if the ship had rolled over on top of him. He thrust his hands up and yelled, "No!" He'd surfaced with his head in a metal mop bucket. Miner couldn't believe it. He almost had to laugh: *The whole Pacific Ocean, and I come up in a bucket!* He chucked it aside. And then he began swimming, hard. He was confident that a distress message had left the ship, and he told himself that rescue had to be on its way.

~

In fact, in a radio shack on the island of Leyte, 650 miles to the west, the message had gotten through. It was received by a sailor named Clair B. Young, on security duty near the sleeping quarters of one Commodore Jacob Jacobson, the ranking officer of the Leyte naval base.

Young read the message by flashlight and quickly realized that it needed to be brought to the commodore's immediate attention. The message announced that the USS *Indianapolis* had been torpedoed and gave her coordinate positions. Young hurried inside Jacobson's hut.

Jacobson was asleep under an umbrella of mosquito netting.

Young turned his flashlight on the commodore's face and announced, "I have a radio message for you, sir."

Jacobson roused himself and, rising on one elbow, read the message by the flashlight's beam.

"Do you have a reply, sir?" Young finally asked.

"No reply at this time," the man said. "If any further messages are received, notify me at once." He sent Young away. Confused, the sailor returned to his post. No effort was made either to confirm or to deny the SOS's legitimacy.

(Several days later, Young would notice that the *Indy* had been assigned a berth in the Leyte harbor. He would notice as well that she hadn't yet shown up in that berth. Remembering the radio message, he was puzzled, but said nothing because, as he later explained, he knew that other people were aware of the SOS, too. In other words, as a lowly enlisted sailor, he felt his hands were tied and that his opinion would matter little.)

A second message was also received at Leyte, according to a sailor named Donald Allen. Allen was serving as a jeep driver for the acting commander of the Philippine Sea Frontier, Commodore Norman Gillette. Gillette oversaw all naval operations on the island.

Shortly after midnight on July 30, a radioman in the officer of the day's Quonset hut, where Allen was standing guard duty, announced that he had just received a distress message. It was from the *Indy* and listed her coordinates. In response, an officer on duty then dispatched two fast, oceangoing navy tugs from the Leyte harbor, bound for the site of the sinking.

At the time, Commodore Gillette himself was playing bridge on the nearby island of Samar, north of Leyte, with a group of officers. According to Allen, later that night, upon hearing that the tugs had been dispatched without his authority, Gillette recalled them to the harbor. No further investigation was made to determine if indeed a ship was sinking.

Finally, a third message was received aboard a landing craft in the Leyte harbor. A sailor named Russell Hetz was on watch when the ship's radio room received an SOS dispatch from a ship claiming to be the USS *Indianapolis*. Eight and a half minutes later, Hetz's ship received a duplicate message. The radio crew tried contacting the *Indy* but couldn't get a response. (Woods and Miner had already abandoned ship.) Hetz's vessel forwarded the message, presumably to the Leyte naval operating base, but it was ignored.

(Clair B. Young's account didn't come to light until 1955. That year, after reading a *Los Angeles Times* story and a subsequent *Saturday Evening Post* article about the sinking, Young was surprised to learn that no record existed of anyone receiving the *Indy*'s SOS. Young wrote to the Navy Department, which replied that the *Post* story, in particular, was "an account of an individual survivor, and not sponsored in all its facts and conclusions by the U.S. Navy." Russell Hetz and Donald Allen made their recollections public in 1998/1999, as the survivors were working in Congress to exonerate Captain McVay.)

The prevailing protocol within naval command was that messages that couldn't be confirmed by a reply were to be disregarded as pranks. The Japanese forces, hoping to confuse U.S. intelligence and draw out search vessels, had made a habit of broadcasting bogus distress signals. Earlier in the war, such a message might have been investigated, but tonight it was written off as a potentially deadly move in the war game.

No help was coming to the *Indy*.

7

SURVIVORS, DRIFTING APART

Early morning hours, July 30

Shortly after the distress calls were sent, Captain McVay found himself alone, leaning against a bulkhead near the port rail. He debated the merits of going down with the ship and considered the immense guilt that he would feel if he were one of the few to survive.

McVay also dreaded the drilling he knew he'd face from naval command once he was back on shore. A captain's primary responsibility is his ship's well-being. McVay understood that, ultimately, he was to blame for the screaming and moaning he heard rising in the night. Yet the sinking had been so quick that he still couldn't understand it. All the normal response systems had collapsed almost immediately. It was like a nightmare he couldn't wake from.

He climbed onto the rail and stood perched above the Pacific. Well, he thought, this is the end of me. Without warning, the captain was brushed off the ship by a tall wave moving along the submerging rails. Looking up from the water, he could see a propeller overhead, and it looked as if the ship might fall on top of him. And then he started swimming through the hot, spilled oil, feeling it burn the back of his neck.

~

It would later be estimated that three hundred men died immediately during the torpedoing and subsequent explosions. Close to nine hundred made it off the ship.

The men surrounded the sinking ship in dog paddling throngs and watched with horrified fascination as the ship stood straight, its bow underwater and its stern sticking up toward the sky. The *Indy* paused, trembling, then began to sink. The ship went down slowly at first, then picking up speed. Within fifteen seconds, the entire bulk of the ship disappeared. All that remained was a wide swath of debris, about half the length of a football field, boiling with foam. The foam itself hissed, like an immense swarm of bees.

There were no stars, just the occasional flash of a crescent moon. At times, the exhausted men floated in complete darkness, unable to discern any horizon at all, the sea rising and falling in heavy swells. At other moments, the sailors were lit by a ghostly silver light from the moon. The living prayed out loud while the dying screamed.

Beneath the men, beneath their kicking feet, the ship was falling as if in slow motion, its bow aimed at the bottom of the sea. A porthole or two still glowed from within, the last flickering remnants of the numerous fires raging through her compartments.

At some point, the pressure became more than the ship could bear, and the *Indy* began self-destructing under her own weight. Air chambers, bulkheads, gas tanks, and boilers—anything that hadn't exploded—now belched, releasing more gas and debris into the diving ship's slipstream.

Completely submerged, the ship let loose one last tremendous explosion, a resounding *whumpfff*. She was falling in three and a half miles of water, some of the deepest on the planet, and it took nearly five minutes for her to reach the bottom.

~

Giles McCoy could feel this last explosion reverberating in his bones, his gut. He was swimming harder than he'd ever swum in his life, trying desperately to flee the ship as she plummeted to the bottom of the sea.

As he swam, he felt something reach out and grab his left leg and tug off his shoe. And then it jerked him backward, pulling him underwater, dragging him down deep. The last thing he remembered before blacking out was the rush of water past his face and the sensation that his eyes were ready to pop under the increasing pressure.

When he snapped back to consciousness, McCoy found himself shooting to the surface at great speed, like a man in an express elevator. He was not in an elevator, though. He was in an air bubble, a huge one. The bubble was clamped around the lower half of his body, leaving his head and shoulders sticking out as he rocketed upward.

He erupted with such force that he rose three feet out of the water. With a splash, he fell back into a black world of screaming men. All around him, the sea was littered with crates of potatoes, ammunition cans, stray life vests, and dead bodies.

The marine private looked around and thought: *Am I gonna live, or will I die?*

~

As the sailors floated through the inky murk of the night, even the most lucid of the *Indy*'s survivors found themselves in an extreme state of disorientation. Without the ship as a point of reference, they had little idea of where they were headed, or how far they had traveled, or how many of their crewmates had made it off alive.

In fact, they were floating now in a slightly southwesterly course. Their intended destination of Leyte lay approximately 650 miles nearly due west. Behind them, maybe another 650 miles to the east, was Guam, their previous port of call. They were drifting through the dead middle of a no-man's-land, a pocket of ocean that spanned some 10,000 square miles.

And they were spread along a roughly three-mile-long line that was lengthening—and widening—by the minute. During the first several hours, the majority of the men had collected in several groups, all scattering in different directions. Each was separated by about a mile of an oily, pitching sea.

Initially, no group knew for certain that any other existed, but as time passed, the scared men would find themselves separated from one cluster and then united with another. Gradually, commands of sorts were evolving.

~

HAYNES'S GROUP

Dr. Haynes and Father Conway found themselves in charge of the largest group of survivors. They were assisted by Marine Captain Edward Parke, a strong man with sandy hair, blue eyes, and a barrel chest. Most of the sailors in this group were in life vests and some in inflatable life belts; Haynes would come to think of them as his "swimmers." Along with Parke and Conway, he set about collecting the men, shouting orders that all sailors within earshot should swim to him.

Bob Gause, hearing the doctor's high-pitched cry, moved toward the sound. Gause was in serious pain, having jumped forty feet from the stern of the ship before she went down, only to hit the massive steel rudder. He didn't think he'd broken any bones, but he could barely swim.

Many of the men were bleeding, vomiting, and overcome with diarrhea. Quite a few had broken legs and arms; some had fractured backs and skulls. Those too seriously damaged by the explosions had already drowned. Haynes, wearing only his cotton pajama pants and life vest, paddled through the wailing crowd, trying to help.

Haynes knew that the men, when in good health, could live for maybe thirty days without food and perhaps seven without water. But the severely weakened and wounded among them, he guessed, had only hours. Rescue had to come soon.

About half of the nine hundred survivors had gotten off the ship with either a life vest or an inflatable life belt. The latter proved worthless as the fuel oil ate into the seams and they started to leak. The men wearing them began to sink and, if they were too weak to swim, to drown. Those without belts or life vests dog-paddled frantically about, keeping lookout: Whenever a boy died, he was flocked by several others eager to take his vest.

Father Conway and Dr. Haynes spent the bleak early morning hours swimming back and forth among these terrified crew members. Sometimes they dragged loners back to the growing mass using an awkward, modified sidestroke. At one point, Parke spotted what looked like a blinking red light. He froze. "Nobody signal back!" he shouted in a hoarse whisper. The marine worried that the light was from the sub that had sunk them. If it found them, they were dead men. They'd be machine-gunned for sure. Then the red light faded. Had it even been real? the sailors wondered.

~

TWIBLE'S GROUP

The second-largest group was led by Ensign Harlan Twible and Chief Engineer Richard Redmayne. It numbered about 325 men, most of whom had jumped from the *Indy* after the Haynes group. The Twible-Redmayne group had left the ship from the flooded rails of the starboard side, which was awash with precious lifesaving equipment. Most of these men had been lucky enough to grab hold of something. They had five floater nets, four rafts, and a smattering of random supplies. These included some malted milk tablets (meant to slake and ease their thirst), biscuits in watertight tins, and a few wooden beakers of potable water.

Four of the five floater nets were piled with the wounded, while the fifth was commandeered as a rest station for the healthy. Each net held about fifty men, none very comfortably (this was twice the recommended number). Every shifting body upset the balance of the whole, causing the sailors to knock heads and slip under the waves bucking beneath them. It was miserable.

~

McVAY

Captain McVay found himself paddling alone through the dark, and it unnerved him. He didn't want to believe that he'd been the only man to survive the sinking, and yet, above the slap and slosh of the waves in his face, he heard no shouts. At this same time, about a mile away, Private McCoy, clutching a life vest he hadn't had time to put on, was bobbing on the oily tide and repeatedly vomiting. He, too, didn't know where he was.

All the groups were traveling in a prevailing westerly equatorial current that was pushing ahead at a steady pace of about one mile an hour. The rate of drift was such that the men would average about twenty-four miles per day. This put the nearest body of land, an island called Mindanao, about three weeks ahead of them. They would never survive that long.

However, the factor that truly determined each group's direction and speed of travel was something called the leeway effect. This phenomenon involves the relationship between exposed body surface, ocean current, and wind. For instance, if a survivor had more of his body submerged in the water than exposed to the wind, the current acted upon him to a greater degree than the trade winds. This meant that those strapped and sunk up to their chests in life vests were typically more affected by the current. Those sitting high in rafts were more forcefully pushed and tugged about by the breezes rather than the ocean.

In between these two groups were McCoy and McVay. They fought through the choppy sea, using every ounce of energy to stay alive.

8

IS THERE A DOCTOR?

Just before dawn, July 30

Almost none of the men adrift knew anything about survival at sea. All were without sails or means to make sails. Only a few of the twelve rafts had functional paddles. There was no compass.

As the sailors drifted through the predawn darkness, the temperature was already rising by the hour. No one knew what would happen next, yet most remained hopeful that sometime in the next forty-eight hours this unbelievable ordeal would be over. They believed that when the *Indy* failed to show in Leyte at its scheduled time of arrival the next day, search parties would be dispatched. They told themselves and one another that rescue was imminent. They told themselves they could be in Leyte in less than two days—and out of the water before that. They prayed aloud for this.

~

McCOY'S GROUP

Private McCoy cursed and struggled to regain his wits. He knew that he was a marine, and that he was expected to be tougher than any of the raw navy sailors.

Up ahead, he could make out a life raft and decided it was a far better place to spend this Monday morning than drifting alone in his life vest. As he prepared to swim to the raft, a shipmate slid up to him, completely taking him by surprise. The boy was in bad shape. He didn't have a life vest, and he was straddling a gunpowder can about the size of a paint bucket.

McCoy looked at him. "We're gonna have to get you a life vest."

"I know."

"Well, we'll just wait for something to float by."

"Where you headed?"

"Over to that yonder raft."

"No, you stay here," said the boy. "They'll be picking us up any minute."

"Like hell." McCoy, who wished for a moment that he'd let the kid keep believing, took off. He tried stroking through the oil-covered sea to the raft, but the film was at least two inches thick. He could barely push through it in his sodden life vest. He struggled back to the boy, spitting out oil.

"I can't make it," the boy said.

"I see that," said McCoy. At that moment, a dead body drifted out of the darkness and continued past them, as if on a mission of its own. McCoy couldn't tell who it was; the face was smeared with oil. He paused, then gingerly reached out, pulled the corpse close, and removed the dead man's life vest. Then he gave the body a gentle push. It sank beneath the waves and was gone.

McCoy handed the vest to the sailor, and tried to figure out the next right move. He could hear yelling from the direction of the raft. "Over here, over here!" they kept shouting. "We got a raft!"

McCoy thought they sounded like they wanted company, and he didn't blame them. As his legs dangled free beneath the surface, he felt that at any second something was about to grab at them again. Suddenly, he tore off his life vest and tossed it to the boy. Then he took an enormous gulp of air and started swimming.

McCoy dived deep and bobbed up every ten feet or so to breathe. He figured it was about one hundred yards to the raft, but it was tough going. By the time he'd drawn close, he was gasping and nearly unconscious. His arms flailed until he finally grabbed hold of a line hanging from the craft's side. He hung there, choking on the oil and staring at his hand, as if disembodied from it. Slowly, he watched it open and release the line. Then he began to sink.

It was at this moment that he felt somebody grab him by the hair and yank him aboard. He rolled over, vomiting, and then he turned to the horrific-looking collection of men before him. McCoy was shocked to see one man so badly burned that the skin was stripped from his arms. The boy's pain was so intense that no sound was coming from his open mouth as he stared up at the sky.

McCoy stuck his finger down his own throat and started vomiting again, attempting to purge his system of the fuel oil and seawater.

On the raft were four other sailors, all vomiting as well. The raft itself was a six-by-ten-foot rectangle of balsa wood stretched with gray canvas. It was already wrecked. Half the bow was gone, and the wood latticework floor was in pieces. Its floor was suspended off the frame on lines that let it hang about five feet beneath the ocean's surface. McCoy wasn't so much sitting on the thing as he was standing up in it, his arms draped over the side.

McCoy couldn't at first identify any of the men because they were all smeared in oil. He could barely remember his own name. Gradually, as he wiped the oil from his eyes, he took in the strange scene. In one corner was a tall, rawboned youth by the name of Bob Brundige, a cotton farmer's son from Tennessee who was maybe nineteen. He silently eyed McCoy from behind his black mask of oil. McCoy simply could not bear to look at his baleful eyes.

In another corner of the raft was a thin, soft-spoken sailor from North Carolina named Felton Outland, eighteen, and one of the ship's antiaircraft gunners. Felton had walked off the ship without even getting his hair wet. But then, like McCoy, he'd been sucked deep underwater by the vacuum of the sinking ship and he'd nearly drowned. He was fully dressed, in a long-sleeved denim shirt and dungarees, his white pillbox sailor hat stuffed in one of his pockets. He appeared unhurt.

Also aboard the raft were nineteen-year-old Ed Payne, a farmer's son from Kentucky, and Willis Gray, about twenty-eight, from Chicago. Payne and Gray, shivering in the pitching raft, were dressed only in T-shirts and dungarees. Both had scrambled from their bunks in enlisted men's country and didn't have time to fully dress before jumping off the ship.

"All right, loosen up," McCoy announced. "We're gonna get picked up in the morning just as soon as they find us missing at Leyte. Okay? So let's keep a sunny side up to this situation!"

Tied to this raft were three more life rafts, each trailing the other on ten-foot lines, making a total of seventeen sailors in the group. In the raft immediately behind McCoy's was Coxswain Mike Kuryla, who had also nearly drowned in the sinking ship's suction. With every passing wave, all four rafts collided. Each collision knocked the men against the rails, or pitched them forward on the submerged flooring, where they sunk before shooting up again, spluttering.

Kuryla was retching but looked like he felt better than McCoy. Kuryla had found his raft a half hour earlier, and his shouts had helped lead Payne, Outland, Brundige, and Gray to the relative safety of theirs. Kuryla reached over the side and plucked up what looked like a greasy black ball. Rubbing off the covering, he discovered it was an onion coated in fuel. He tucked it inside his vest for safekeeping.

McCoy was able to scavenge a tin of malted milk tablets from a passing wave. But, rooting around in the raft itself, he found nothing useful whatsoever. He badly wanted to get his hands on a signal mirror or some flares. Ravenous, McCoy tried eating one of the malted milk tablets, but they just made him thirstier; his lips and tongue were already dry as a bone.

Clearly, things were going from bad to worse. The young marine resolved to take action: He would clean his pistol. Reaching down into the water inside the raft, he found his holster still attached to the belt on his fatigues. He removed the .45 and held it up in the air, shaking the water from the barrel. McCoy could disassemble and reassemble the weapon blindfolded, and that was essentially what he tried to do now. He guessed that he and his raft mates would need it sooner or later to signal a passing plane or a rescue ship.

McCoy told everyone to hold out their hands, then placed a gun part in each outstretched palm. Using his T-shirt, he wiped the oil from the receiver and grip—it was a poor cleaning job, at best. When a tin of petroleum jelly floated by, he snatched it and eagerly greased the action on the pistol.

McCoy racked a round and announced that the gun was clean. Then he spotted something floating on the horizon—something huge and gray. It was heading directly for them.

McCoy became convinced that it was a ship, and he was certain that it was coming to rescue them. He raised his pistol and fired off a shot. The gun's sound was instantly swallowed by the air. McCoy peered anxiously into the dark, hoping to see a return flash from the ship, some signal he'd been spotted. Nothing—he saw nothing.

"What's wrong with these people!" He racked another round, then fired again.

"Why don't they see us!" And then McCoy had an awful thought: What if whatever he was shooting at started shooting back? He suddenly realized that the silhouette might be a sub. Or maybe a Japanese destroyer.

Giles McCoy felt dumber than he'd ever felt in his life. He wondered if he had lost his senses without even knowing it; he knew he had to keep a close check on his feelings, his actions. He felt like throwing up again.

~

HAYNES'S GROUP

Dr. Haynes and his group of men were on the verge of collapse. Herding them together had been painstaking work, and it seemed to Haynes they would never get everybody rounded up. The tireless efforts of Father Conway and Captain Parke aside, the sailors were close to scattering in all directions.

"Count off!" Captain Parke bellowed. Parke, the men had always said aboard ship, might give them hell, but he also gave them credit for their efforts as military men. Slowly at first, they began sounding off, until the number grew to four hundred. To Haynes, it was an amazing spectacle of command and endurance on Parke's part. The marine then ordered the men to tie their life jackets together to keep them from drifting apart. It worked. Instinctively, each one wrapped his legs and arms around the boy in front of him. In this way, each one could also lie back on the chest of the boy behind him. Together, they drifted like this, looking up at a blackness.

In the center of this human ring, Dr. Haynes floated in his life vest. Like most of the men, his face was covered in oil. Many of the sailors didn't recognize him. Soon the cries started out, "Hey, anybody seen a doctor? We need a doctor here!"

Haynes considered the request. He knew it would be much easier to hang back, to slink away into the crowd and shirk the responsibility of treating sailors who were really too sick to be helped. The prospect of facing the misery around him without the aid of any medical supplies filled him with dread.

Then he heard a voice: *Your job is to make people better.* It was as if his mother were whispering in his ear. He hadn't thought of her much lately. Now he pictured her with his father in their comfortable house on Fifth Street in Manistee, Michigan. He wondered if she was looking at the lake, and whether it was sunny there. His father would be at his dental practice. When Haynes snapped out of the reverie, he realized what he needed to do.

A few men were vomiting so violently that they were actually doing somersaults in the water. Trying to keep calm, Haynes called out: "Here! Right here! Where is the sick sailor?" And then he moved into the throng. About a dozen sailors were holding a body aloft. It was an incredible feat of strength considering they were all treading water furiously to stay afloat beneath the added weight.

The man in question was in terrible shape. His eyes had been burned away. The flesh on his hands was gone, and what remained were bare tendons. The sailors held him in an effort to keep these wounds out of the stinging bath of salt water.

Haynes recognized the man as his good friend and liberty buddy, Gunnery Officer Stanley Lipski. Miraculously, Lipski had made his way blind from the quarterdeck, off the ship, and into the water. Haynes knew that Lipski's pain must be intolerable—he himself could barely look at his old friend, who was moaning softly. Stanley, he knew, was one tough bird. Haynes also understood that his friend didn't have long to live. Reluctantly, he turned away to those he could actually help.

The horizon glowed with a faint bloom of sunrise. Dr. Haynes prayed that daylight would comfort the men.

9

BUMPS IN THE WATER

All day and night, July 30

McVAY'S GROUP

Floating to the northeast of both Haynes and McCoy, Captain McVay was formulating his own plan for survival. Other than the oil in his eyes, he was neither injured nor in other physical distress. He was actually in remarkably good shape. Even his wristwatch was still working perfectly. He was, however, unable to shake the fear that he was the only one to have made it off the ship alive.

Then something nudged him. It was a potato crate. He hopped on top and grasped it between his legs, continuing to scope the horizon. But he still couldn't see any other survivors.

McVay could hear voices in the distance, though. Two life rafts drifted toward him from the darkness, and he stroked over atop his potato crate. Finding the rafts empty, he climbed aboard one of them and quickly lashed it to the other. Out of the night came a yell: "Help! Anybody out there!"

"Yes! It's the captain here!" Bearing down on the paddle, he rowed ahead to meet three blackened, indistinguishable faces. He pulled a quartermaster named Vincent Allard aboard his own raft, and then hauled the other two sailors into the second.

McVay knew Allard well. At thirty-three, the quartermaster had served on the *Indy* for three years—since the ship's early days of the Aleutian Islands bombardment at the beginning of the Pacific war—under five different captains. A quartermaster served his captain in the daily enforcement of the ship's regulations, and this morning McVay had never been happier to see him.

With Allard were two other sailors. Then, twenty minutes later another raft with five men aboard drifted toward McVay.

"Boys," McVay said, surveying his motley crew, "is this all that's left of us?" John Spinelli, a cook from New Mexico, didn't have an answer. Only several hours earlier, he'd been playing a little after-hours pinochle with his buddies in the bakeshop, a pan of fresh rolls cooling on the table. And then his world had sunk beneath him. But being in McVay's presence was a huge comfort.

McVay took command of the three rafts, one floater net, and eight sailors—a ragtag flotilla that he intended to lead, nonetheless, with unbending fairness and sturdy naval discipline. "Don't worry," he told the crew, "we will be rescued—don't lose faith. Keep heart."

The words rang hollow; McVay realized that there was no guarantee rescue would come anytime soon. He hoped that the pilots of the planes that he'd requested to meet him for gunnery practice on Tuesday morning, July 31, near Leyte would report their failure to show. If they didn't report the ship missing, McVay further reasoned, and if no one had received their SOS, rescue would begin when the *Indy* didn't show up in port at Leyte midday on Tuesday.

With this in mind, he told his group that Thursday seemed the earliest date they could hope for aid. He confidently announced that it would be ships, not planes, that would find them. "Planes," he explained, "would be flying too high to ever see us."

All the men, though bone-weary and scared, felt good about their chances.

~

TWIBLE'S GROUP

At dawn, when the sun launched off the horizon and began its race into the sky, the temperature shot from a nighttime cool of low 80s to over 100 degrees. Just 12 degrees north of the equator, the heat was merciless. The men's exposed heads baked as they squinted in agony and paddled about.

The large group led by Ensign Harlan Twible and Richard Redmayne seemed to have everything it needed to survive. They had life rafts, floater nets, and food—but lacked cohesion among their ranks. Unlike the group headed by Haynes, Parke, and Father Conway, which was performing as one unit bent on survival, this group was mostly an uneasy collection of alienated souls. Redmayne had been badly burned in the explosions, and although he was an officer, he was not in a position to command.

Ensign Twible tried to compensate, but he was seriously under-experienced. Still, he had taken to heart his Naval Academy training, and he began a close imitation of what he believed an officer's behavior should be. More than three hundred oil-smeared faces stared back at Twible when he issued his first order. As he told them to tie their life vests together, the blank look in their eyes startled him. Few obeyed.

Then, from within the crowd, a voice said, "You heard the officer. Now do it!" This was Durward Horner, a gunnery captain, one of the old salts who was widely respected by the crew.

Twible spotted one of the sailors holding up a bottle of whiskey. He couldn't believe it—what had the boy been thinking as he struggled to get off the ship? "Toss that out," Twible ordered. "It'll only cause you trouble."

The sailor grumpily handed the bottle over and Twible emptied it into the sea.

Jack Miner—minus the bucket that had fallen on his head earlier—was in a daze, but he tried to do as commanded. As

Twible was issuing an order to remove shoes so as to swim more easily, Miner looked down and saw something flash beneath his feet. One moment the image was there, and then it was gone. He gave it no more thought.

~

About two miles to the south of this group, Dr. Haynes, Captain Parke, and Father Conway were undeterred by the day's scorching heat. One of their men found a life ring and passed it to Parke, who quickly devised a use for it. Attached to the ring was two hundred feet of ship's line. Parke ordered the sailors—as many as would fit—to grab hold. As if impelled by an invisible wind, the line began curling around the epicenter of the life ring.

Captain Parke ordered Haynes into the center among the wounded. Father Conway paddled the edges, hearing confessions and saying last rites for those too wounded to carry on.

About half the men were naked or dressed only in their underwear, while others wore only a shirt or just their shoes. Some had nothing but a hat. Still, the men's spirits rose as the day progressed, and they cheerfully cursed their predicament. Having endured the torpedoing, the group was plagued by a strange giddiness. At times, they laughed and shouted over one another's heads like men at a New Year's Eve party. Rescue, most were sure, was just a day, maybe two, away.

~

Around 10:00 a.m., Twible and his group unexpectedly drifted free of the vaporous oil slick. Beneath them the sea lit up like an enormous green room. The effect was fantastic. Suddenly they were floating in space, suspended between earth and sky. A complex web of sea life, including giant grouper, man-of-war jellyfish with stinging tentacles, and giant barracudas, swam beneath them.

But the relief was short-lived. The sea also teemed with dozens of probing bacteria and organisms that, as the men drifted, began gnawing at their flesh. The salt water itself was a caustic brew, consisting of 3.5 percent sodium chloride, and including trace elements of sulphate, magnesium, potassium, bicarbonate, and boric acid. Floating in it was not unlike immersion in a mild acid bath. The sailors swallowed small amounts of seawater each time a wave splashed their faces. The high potassium levels in each taste began leaking into their bloodstreams. This caused a breakdown in their red blood cells leading to increased physical weakness.

Whenever the men inhaled any of the salt spray, accidentally aspirating it, it set off what doctors call a "plasma shift" in the lungs. This meant that their lungs were slowly beginning to fill with fluid, the accumulation of which could cause the onset of pulmonary edema. This damage to the lungs would lead to difficulty in breathing, a lowering of the oxygen content in the bloodstream, and finally rapid, irregular heartbeats.

By late morning the heavy swell dropped and the sea went flat. The sun began shattering around them in millions of burning medallions across the water. The sailors' eyes stung in the glare. For some, the pain was unbearable. Even with their eyes closed, they could still see the sun. Each blink of an eyelid felt like sandpaper dragged over the inflamed cornea.

Dr. Haynes ordered them to tear their clothing in strips and tie them in blindfolds. As they drifted, they now resembled men facing a firing squad. Haynes knew the situation with the sun was bad, but thought it would be controlled if the men kept their eyes protected. He also noticed that the whites of some of the men's eyes were swelling from exposure to the salt water.

Haynes's sense of futility defied his paternal instincts and determination as a doctor. He knew that, by the hour, the sailors could turn into physiological time bombs, detonating all around him.

He knew that he was no different from the rest.

~

McVAY'S GROUP

Captain McVay and his ragged crew passed Monday morning in relative comfort, all things considered. The nine men hunched down on the edges of their rafts. At some point they discovered that the fuel oil, which had nearly poisoned them, made an excellent sunblock. McVay ordered them to slather it on any exposed parts of their bodies.

As the day went on, planes buzzed high overhead, some near, some far. In spite of McVay's earlier pronouncement that rescue would in all probability not arrive by air, the planes were a welcome sight and gave hope to the captain and sailors. Whenever one passed, McVay ordered everyone to splash and kick at the water, in a fruitless bid to attract attention.

At 1:00 p.m., McVay spotted what he thought was a twin-engine bomber flying west. He flashed it with a metal signal mirror, but to no avail. At 3:00 p.m., he saw what he identified as either a B-24 or a B-29 passing to the south. It also failed to respond to the signal mirror. These planes had taken off from Tinian and Okinawa and were almost certainly heading toward the Philippines.

McVay patiently instructed the men in the use of the signal mirror and the flares. But as more planes passed overhead, these proved of no use. This shocked some of the men, but not the captain.

"It's the same old thing," he announced. "If an aviator doesn't expect to see anything, he doesn't see it. He's too busy flying his plane."

McVay also took an inventory of the sailors' rations. He found several cans of Spam and of crackers, a couple of tins of malted milk tablets, a first aid kit, flares, a flare gun, and a fishing kit containing hooks and line. There was enough, he figured, to last ten days at sea. He ordered the crew to stand two-hour watches for rescue planes.

At one point, he spotted a wooden water cask drifting on the tide and hauled it aboard. It was a boon worth its weight in gold, and the men were overjoyed. Sadly, McVay realized that the wooden keg had cracked. Still, he shook it and heard the jostle of liquid inside. He gingerly lifted it to his lips and sipped. The taste was awful; it contained plain salt water. But sensing how vulnerable the sailors were, he lowered the cask and smiled. The water, he told them, was okay, but that they would save it for a time when they really needed a drink. He then encouraged them to keep their eyes peeled for planes.

This was a characteristic moment for the captain. On board the *Indy*, he had once made his reputation with the enlisted men by standing in the sailors' chow line. The officers normally ate at their own mess, but McVay had heard the men complaining about the food. He was determined to taste it himself. After the cook carefully dolloped the slop onto the captain's dented metal tray, McVay sat down and ate. It wasn't terrible. It was mediocre, which in McVay's world may have been an even worse offense. He got up, approached the cooks, and announced: "These men work hard for this ship. You make sure they eat damn well. I don't want to hear any more complaints."

~

Below, drawn up from the deep, perhaps attracted by the booming of the *Indy*'s exploding chambers or lured by the blood trail of the injured and the dead, the sailors' greatest fears were coming to life.

By dusk on Monday, hundreds of sharks had encircled them. There were makos, tigers, whitetips, and blues. Rising at the speed of a man at a gentle run, the sharks ascended from the depths of the dark sea. The men, lying in their rafts, hanging from floating nets, and bobbing in life vests, began to feel things bumping from below. They mistook the nudges and kicks for the touch of their comrades treading water.

The sailors nodded off and slept, if their wounds allowed them to rest. They woke often, with a start, staring into the dark, wondering, *Who's there?*

10

SHARK ATTACKS

Morning, Tuesday, July 31

The sharks attacked around dawn on Tuesday, July 31.

McCoy looked over his raft's edge and saw them prowling in frenzied schools. Like figures trapped in glass, the huge, gray fish were spiraling to the surface.

They had begun their attacks late Sunday night, but in the dark, many of the disoriented survivors hadn't really taken notice. Around daybreak on Monday, McCoy had seen a man slumped in his life vest—apparently asleep—suddenly disappear. McCoy waited for the vest to pop back up to the surface, but it never did.

In all likelihood, the sharks now gathered around the men had been following the *Indy* for days. It is the habit of sharks to track oceangoing vessels and feed on refuse regularly tossed overboard. The *Indy*, made of steel, emitted low-grade electrical currents that may have stimulated and attracted the predators.

Until this point, it seemed, the restless fish had been feeding mostly on the dead, tearing at the bodies as they fell to the ocean floor. Or they had concentrated on lone, straying swimmers. But now the sharks were starting to home in on the large groups. Those sailors who were naked or not fully clothed were at greatest risk of attack. The fish keyed in on color contrasts, such as that between a pale body and a blue sea.

Sharks are some of the oldest predators on the planet, dating back four hundred million years. No evidence has ever been found that sharks prefer humans to their regular diet of fish. Nor has it been scientifically established that they attack wounded or bleeding people more readily than the unwounded. Biologists are not even sure why sharks attack humans, although they do believe that people emit irregular low-level frequencies and odors that resemble those of wounded fish.

~

In Dr. Haynes's group this Tuesday, one sailor woke from sleep and gave the buddy next to him a "good morning" shove. The guy didn't respond. When the sailor pushed again, the friend's body tipped over like a child's toy and bobbed away. He'd been eaten in half, right up to the hem of his life vest.

At one point, Bob Gause swam away from the group to aid

an exhausted sailor who was on the verge of drowning. He was waving his hands and calling for help. As Gause paddled out, he was intercepted immediately by a large dorsal fin knifing toward him, so he swam as fast as he could back to the group. The boy in distress soon disappeared.

As the shark attacks multiplied, the once optimistic sailors were filled with a sense of helplessness. Sailor Jack Cassidy came face-to-face with a tiger shark that had been bothering him so long that he had even given it a name. He called the beast Oscar. He swung at it with his homemade knife and buried the blade an inch deep in the fish's tough snout, but Oscar swam away as if only annoyed. Cassidy was furious—he wanted to *kill* the shark—but he was relieved to be left alone.

As the water flashed with twisting tails and dorsal fins, the men resolved to stay calm. They clamped their hands over their ears against the erupting screams. But this resolve vanished when one of the sailors was dragged through the water like a fisherman's bobber tugged by a big catfish. The victim, clenched in the uplifted jaws of a shark, was pushed at waist level through the surf, screaming.

Others disappeared quietly without a trace, their life vests shooting back to the surface empty, the straps in shreds. As the excited sharks grew more agitated, the attacks intensified in ferocity.

Capable of bursts of speed up to forty-three miles per hour, the sharks were attacking using what are known as "bump-and-bite maneuvers." The bumps stun the prey, while the bites deliver the victims to eternity.

~

About twenty-five sharks circled around McCoy's group of rafts. Most, he estimated, measured about ten feet. He watched as they searched the rafts looking for a way in, pursuing them the way wolves follow the scent trail of a wounded deer. Because McCoy's raft was broken at the bow, there was, in fact, a gaping entrance. He and his four compatriots bunched together at the far end of the craft as one shark rose up through the broken wooden grating in the floor.

McCoy recoiled as the shark's pointed snout, tipped with large black nasal chambers, jabbed hungrily through the hole. The eyes reminded him of plums. The teeth, about two inches long, were snow-white, protruding from a jaw about two feet wide.

At first McCoy was stunned by his fear. He reached for his .45 in its holster and pulled the trigger, but the gun wouldn't fire. Then he kicked out blindly, trying to drive the fish from the raft with his leg. The rough scaly skin ripped at his bare foot, but he managed to kick the fish in the eye. McCoy was amazed as he watched it thrashing back out of the raft in retreat. Glancing over the side, he watched the shark writhe and spin fifteen feet below him. But within seconds another shark came nosing into the raft's opening.

Elsewhere, in Dr. Haynes's group, some of the men went perfectly still during the attacks, while others flailed. Men at the edges of a floating group fared worse than those in the middle.

Clinging to a floater net, one sailor looked down and saw hundreds of sharks circling.

Around Captain McVay's raft, one particular shark passed so close that the men tried knocking the pilot fish leading it with a paddle. They hoped to capture the small pilot fish and eat it. When they realized they couldn't kill fish, they swung at the shark itself. It was an enormous twelve-footer. The blow didn't deter the shark. Instead, it circled the raft in ever-tightening rings, at times bumping the raft's bottom with its dorsal fin.

And then, just as quickly as they began, the attacks stopped, the ghostly shapes dropping back into the gloom beneath.

This pattern of attacks in low-light conditions, particularly at twilight and in the dawn hours, soon established itself as the rhythm of the men's days. The sharks would attack in the morning, then cruise through the wounded and the dying all day, feeding again at night on the living.

~

By midmorning Tuesday, the sailors were deeply bewildered and distraught. Their thinking now wasn't so much about being rescued. They just wanted to survive the sharks.

In the nearly thirty-six hours since the sinking, the Haynes group had drifted ahead of the middle of the pack by about one mile. About four miles to the north, were McCoy and his group of four rafts. About four miles east, Captain McVay and his four rafts, one net, and nine men floated. Trailing McVay by about one mile was the largest group of rafters and survivors perched atop floater nets, led by Twible and Redmayne.

The four groups of men now covered about twelve miles of ocean, and they were drifting farther and farther apart.

As the sharks rampaged through Haynes's group the rough tails ripped abrasions in the sailors' dangling legs. Dehydrated, their raw skin leached of its protective oils by immersion, their bodies were turning rubbery. The bleeding attracted smaller tropical fish that began to nip at the exposed pieces of flesh, while at the same time, barracudas began flashing about. It seemed to the men that everything around them wanted them dead. Even the thick, humid air of the afternoon choked those suffering from the onset of pneumonia.

Dr. Haynes paddled up to find one man staring longingly into his trembling hands, at the winking jewel of water cupped within.

The boy looked up. "Whaddya say, Doc? Just a little sip?"

"No!" Haynes warned. "You can't drink it!"

"C'mon, it can't hurt," whispered the boy.

"It's certain death—do you understand?"

The boy smiled, an inscrutable smirk, and it unnerved Haynes. Finally the boy poured the water out and swam away. Haynes, however, was horrified. He knew that if they began drinking the seawater, they'd start dying in droves.

At this latitude, the Pacific was a steady 85 degrees, warm by most ocean standards. But it was still more than 10 degrees cooler than core body temperature, and since the sinking the men had been turning hypothermic. This condition affected each survivor differently. The more clothing or body fat on a person, the better in terms of heat retention.

On average, the sailors were losing about 1 degree Fahrenheit for every hour of exposure in the water during the nighttime hours. At night the air temperature dropped to the mid-80s from the daytime high near 100.

As soon as the sun set the men started shivering uncontrollably. This was the body's way of generating heat, but it quadrupled the rate of oxygen consumed. Hypothermia depresses the central nervous system as the body slows to conserve energy. At a core temperature of 93 degrees (nearly 5 degrees below normal), speech becomes difficult, apathy develops, and amnesia typically sets in. At around 85 degrees, the kidneys stop filtering the body's waste—urination stops—and hypoxia, or poisoning, commences. Breathing becomes labored, the heart beats raggedly, and consciousness dims. The afflicted fall into an inattentive stupor.

By Tuesday at dawn, Dr. Haynes estimated the core body temperatures of the *Indy*'s men were probably hovering right around 92 degrees. Later, after the shark attack, as the sun rose and baked them, their temperatures began to rise a degree or two. In essence, the sailors had fallen into a pattern of abrupt energy drain and renewal. But increasingly, they were building a deficit that eventually even the heat of day wouldn't be able to erase. With their body temperatures dipping low, the men were wobbling off into the land of fatal judgment.

11

DEADLY ASSUMPTIONS
AND A DEADLY
TEMPTATION

Tuesday, July 31
Leyte and site of sinking

Back on land, some three hundred miles across the Philippine
Sea, the port director's office on Leyte was a busy place this
sunny Tuesday morning. In the harbor, warships from Nimitz's
and MacArthur's fleets were moored, awaiting food servicing
and other resupply.

Carved from jungle scrub by invading U.S. forces, the island's
installation was a grid of gravel roads, Quonset huts, and command posts. Military jeeps roared through scorching heat and
dust, delivering progress reports of the invasion's plans.

On Leyte there were two central posts of command. One was
called the Philippine Sea Frontier, and at that office was a giant

plotting board. An operations officer marked ships' arrivals and departures on this board. This morning, sometime after 11:00, the *Indy*'s scheduled ETA (estimated time of arrival), the officer moved the ship's marker into the "arrived" slot on the board. He assumed her voyage had been uneventful; at least he had heard nothing to the contrary. Combatant vessels were always assumed to have arrived at their destinations, unless contradictory news was announced.

The minutes began piling into hours, and no one noticed that the ship had not docked in the harbor.

No one, that is, except Lieutenant Gibson. The lieutenant was also on the island of Leyte but worked in a different department. Gibson kept his own list and noticed the *Indianapolis* was not among the seventeen ships listed as having shown up on Tuesday. At that point he might have informed his superiors that the *Indy* had not arrived. Instead, he marked the *Indy* as "overdue" and placed her on an "Expected Arrivals and Departures" list for Wednesday, August 1.

Gibson did this because combatant ships like the *Indianapolis* were not under his jurisdiction, but of higher commands. He assumed the *Indianapolis* had been diverted by new orders to another destination.

Out at sea, Vice Admiral Oldendorf, commander of Task Force 95, to whom the *Indy* was to eventually report, also had no reason to be concerned. Oldendorf knew the *Indy* was due to report to him, but assumed details about her ETA were forthcoming.

Likewise, Rear Admiral McCormick, to whom the *Indy* was to report that day in preparation for joining Oldendorf, was unfazed. McCormick assumed the *Indianapolis* had simply changed her course. He knew that combatant ships were regularly diverted from their original orders.

It would have been a two-hour plane trip from one of Leyte's airstrips—or a day's cruise by rescue boat from her harbor—to reach the men, but no one was leaving.

~

By late afternoon, life for the sailors had mutated from horrific to unbearable.

Those with broken arms and legs and backs had gone into shock and died. Others had succumbed to massive bleeding or head wounds that suspended them in a netherworld. Still others simply drowned because they were too exhausted to keep swimming.

They'd been afloat now without food, water, shelter, or sleep for over forty hours. In total, 1,195 crew members, along with Captain McVay's U.S. Naval Academy classmate, Navy Captain Edwin Crouch, who'd boarded the ship at Guam, had set sail days prior. Now, probably no more than 600 were still alive. In the previous twenty-four hours alone, at least 200 had likely slipped beneath the waves or been victims of shark attack.

Since the sinking, each boy had been floating through the hours asking himself the same hard question: *Will I live, or do I quit?* And, as Tuesday unfolded, some of the starved, bleeding, and delirious men began to form their answers. For those who gave up, death now seemed a matter of destiny. They started committing suicide. Those still lucid enough looked on in disbelief as their former shipmates calmly untied their life vests, took a single stroke forward, and sank without a word. Others suddenly turned from the group and started swimming, waiting for a shark to hit. They looked up in terrified satisfaction when it did. Others simply fell face forward and refused to rise.

~

McCOY'S GROUP

McCoy woke with a start to find one less man in his cluster of rafts. The original head count of seventeen had by now dwindled to about twelve. Ed Payne and Willis Gray hovered in and out of consciousness, while Felton Outland and Bob Brundige remained alert. The beating of the rafts together in the swells had enlarged the hole in the floor of McCoy's, and the exposed balsa, its canvas ripped away, was shredding.

There was talk of cutting the rafts loose to put an end to the constant collisions, but the idea frightened the men, who found comfort in one another's presence. McCoy didn't know what to do.

McCoy, drained and hollow-eyed, couldn't take his eyes off the life vest belonging to the boy who'd slipped away from the group during the night. The empty vest spooked McCoy. All its straps were still tightly tied—it looked like some trick that Houdini might've played. Then McCoy peered into the water and got another shock: The boy was floating below him, spread-eagled, about fifteen feet below the surface. He lay motionless until a current caught him; then it was as if he were flying in the depths.

McCoy had never been overly religious; his mom was the spiritual one in the family. But now he began the process of what he'd later call his purification; he started asking God to forgive him for his sins. He was resolved to live but he was also getting ready to die.

Things were becoming increasingly surreal. Nearby, in Mike Kuryla's raft, one sailor in the group had opened his wallet, given away the few dollars inside, and said, "I'll see you, good buddies."

Kuryla had picked up the bills and yelled out, "I'm going to spend this and have a drink on you guys."

But the desperate boy ignored his weary attempt at humor and swam away. He was never seen again.

~

HAYNES'S GROUP

In Dr. Haynes's group, Stanley Lipski had somehow managed to hang on until late the previous night. "Lew, I'm dying," Lipski had finally whispered in Haynes's ear. "Please tell my wife I love her. Tell her I want her to marry again."

Haynes had felt a shocking sense of relief. He cradled his moaning friend in his arms, staring into the sightless black scabs that had been his eyes, and said goodbye.

Around him, Marine Captain Parke moved from man to man. He gave his life vest to a boy without one, and slapped those who looked to be thinking of drowning themselves. The hard-charging marine was spending an enormous amount of time looking for replacement vests, both for others and for himself. Dr. Haynes was worried about him, and about Father Conway. The priest also never stopped swimming among the sailors, hearing their confessions and administering last rites.

~

McVAY'S GROUP

Captain McVay's spirits were threatening to wilt and slip past despair. The realization had sunk in that his absence from this morning's six o'clock meeting with the planes for gunnery practice hadn't triggered a rescue effort. Still, considering the adequate rations, he attempted to remain optimistic about their survival.

"Something's happened," McVay told the sailors. "I don't know what, but they're going to miss us sooner or later." McVay tried fishing for the bonito and mackerel he saw schooling below the raft, but after an enormous shark ripped at his fishing lines and stole his baited hooks, he gave up in disgust.

The captain surveyed what was left of his weary and nauseated crew, perched precariously on the rafts' rails and staring at the burning sky. They were still looking for planes, for any signs of rescue.

"Don't give up, men!" McVay told them constantly. His mind was beginning to cloud with misgivings about his life to come if he ever stepped back ashore. For the men, rescue would be the end of the ordeal. For him, if it came, it would only be the start of another hell—one that would be his alone to bear. He tried to match the strength of the sailors, who were bleeding and suffering without bitterness or complaint. And yet at the same time, he watched them with an increasing sense of guilt. He wondered if they held him responsible for what had happened. McVay had no way of knowing that perhaps the disaster could have been averted if his superiors had shared with him what they had learned through ULTRA, the code-breaking program. The navy top officials never told McVay that they had information that Japanese subs were known to be operating in the very route the *Indy* would be traveling.

At nightfall, the captain gathered the group together and recited the Lord's Prayer. This would be their third night since the sinking.

~

HAYNES'S GROUP

A few miles away Dr. Haynes was desolate, drifting into uncharted territories of pain. Like Marine Captain Parke and Father Conway, he had been paddling for nearly two full days, trying to do his best to encourage the men and sustain their dwindling hopes. By day's end, though, Father Conway was in terrible shape, and Captain Parke was beginning to show signs of total collapse.

Haynes himself was slipping in and out of consciousness, experiencing alternating moments of clarity and confusion. *You have patients to take care of,* he kept reminding himself. He thought of home, of his wife and sons ten thousand miles away. What would they do if he died? The question made survival seem even more essential. But when he snapped back to reality, he slumped deeper into misery and disbelief.

Overhead, more planes—bombers and transports—passed without pause, and Haynes prayed. He prayed that in a few hours they would be discovered, steeling himself against any other thoughts, any other possibilities.

That night the situation at sea took one more precipitous turn. The dehydrated sailors, their tongues swelling, their throats squeezing shut, and their minds unhinging, began drinking salt water. After hours of resisting the temptation, they drank furtively at first, as if ashamed. Then they began to gorge themselves, murmuring in pleasure as they sipped through bleeding lips from the cool mirror of the sea.

Dr. Haynes looked on in horror, his worst fear realized: Soon these men would all be dead. He swam among them, screaming and punching at their faces. But his pleas to stop were ignored. The sailors lifted their dripping chins, regarded him coolly with glazed eyes, then lowered their jaws back to the waiting sea.

As they drank, the men were setting off a complex series of chemical reactions, all of them volatile. The sea contains twice the salinity that the human body can safely ingest. As the men drank, their cells were shrinking, expanding, and exploding as they sacrificed what's called their "free water." This was the cells' attempt to put more water in the bloodstream to lower the sodium content. It was futile.

The sailors' kidneys were also trying to filter the salt out of their blood before dumping it back into the circulatory system. But the kidneys were unable to keep ahead of the sodium tidal wave.

Haynes knew the men were shorting out on salt, succumbing to what in medical terms is known as hypernatremia. One of its most severe symptoms is delirium.

Dr. Haynes would eventually feel helpless as he observed a few of the men foaming at the mouth as their eyes rolled back in their heads. He watched their lips turn blue, heard their breathing grow ragged. In their brains, neurons were misfiring or not firing at all.

Some of the sailors now asked him if they could evaporate the salt from the seawater by cupping it in their hands and holding it up to the sun. He gently shook his head, told them, "No, son," and begged the men to be patient.

Haynes began keeping a close eye on those he knew weren't married or who were without close ties on shore. Those with families, he discovered, were fighting the temptation to drink from the sea.

Those who succumbed fell into violent fits and, finally, comas. At first, they whooped and hollered and spun circles in the water, arms flailing, until finally a kind of explosion took place and they went limp. More than one boy came to rest in a ring of circling sharks. The dead and near-dead floated motionless, facing the sky, bodies jerking, eyes blinking in terror. A few of the poor men clawed the air in thirst or panic. Their throats were too dry to scream. Some of them died in a matter of hours.

It was dark now, and Haynes could feel the anxiety swirling around him. The life vests, the sailors' last line to hope, were growing waterlogged. Some were riding as much as six inches lower in the sea, making it even more difficult not to swallow salt water. The vests possessed an estimated buoyancy limit of forty-eight hours, and they were approaching that limit. After this, the men would be floating on borrowed time. And they knew it.

As Haynes grew feverish and started to shake, he felt his power of reasoning slipping away. Screams shook the night air, the awful music of the savaging as the sharks attacked around the edges of the group. Haynes had yet to see a shark attack close up, but this was almost worse. It was torture; too much was left to his imagination.

He instructed the sailors to tie their vests together and form a protective mass. They obeyed, huddling in moaning clusters as the temperature plummeted. Soon all were shivering uncontrollably. One boy chewed completely through a rope he'd placed between his chattering teeth. It was so cold they began announcing when they had to pee so others could gather around them for the warmth.

It was as if their life before this nightmare had completely slipped away.

12

DELIRIUM IGNITES VIOLENCE

Early morning, Wednesday, August 1

~

Where does a man go when there are no more corners to turn, when he's running out of hope, out of luck, out of time? It was the sailors' third morning in the water and it looked as if not a single one of them would live to see another day. And the situation was about to get worse.

~

HAYNES'S GROUP

In the very early hours of Wednesday, August 1, the men started killing one another. Haynes had spent the night listening to the sounds of shivering and chattering teeth. Then, from somewhere not far off he heard a shout: "There's an enemy here! He's trying to kill me. Get him!"

This was followed by piercing screams, but Haynes had no idea what was causing them. He could see, but barely, sailors fumbling with the knots holding their vests together. Then, suddenly, the circle of men blew apart, as if parted by an invisible wind. They scattered in all directions.

The doctor swam into the pandemonium. He saw men with knives blindly stabbing at buddies who were still tied to them. Those unable to punch or stab rose up and tried to drown the closest breathing thing they could find. One sailor gouged out another's eyes with his fingers.

Haynes understood that the melee was too big for him to stop and he watched in horror as one sailor tried stabbing another, who, in turn, was rescued by two nearby sailors. They jumped atop the sailor with the knife and held him under. As they drowned him, they screamed long, defiant cries of anguish. Then the rescuers turned on each other. Hypothermia, dehydration, hypernatremia, the onset of starvation—Haynes knew that these conditions all caused delirium and were turning the minds of these men inside out. In a matter of ten minutes, an estimated fifty men were killed. The melee had the intensity of a flash fire.

Haynes tried paddling away from the bursts of violence around him, but wherever he went, another fight was raging. Then he was jumped by two gibbering figures carrying knives. As they shoved him deep underwater and held him down, he knew he was drowning. Kicking and punching at his attackers' arms, the doctor managed to break free, shooting to the surface with a wrench.

Swimming away as fast as possible, Haynes kept his eyes trained on his attackers until he reached the fringe of the chaos. He was heartsick; the sailors had become a pack of fighting dogs.

Sharks, he realized, were still circling, and he was certain they were pursuing him. But if he returned to the group, he was sure he would be drowned. So he floated, trying to catch his breath, and attempted to remain perfectly still.

Haynes's mouth was just inches from the surface of the water, which he knew was poison to him. His vest was so waterlogged he wondered how much longer it would hold him up. Even the slightest movement of his hands was a monumental effort—he was that tired. Convinced that he would soon slip beneath the waves, he cried out for help.

Suddenly he heard a voice in his ear: "Easy, Doc," it said, "I've got you."

It was the pharmacist's mate, John Schmueck. He and Haynes had stood aboard the *Indy* watching their helpless patients slide into the sea. Now, Schmueck shoved his arms through Haynes's life vest and hoisted the gasping doctor onto his hip.

"Nothing's gonna happen to you now, Doc," Schmueck said. But Haynes was out cold.

~

Private McCoy had cut himself and his four raft mates free of the other rafts in their group sometime before sunset the previous day. They were now adrift, bucking and gliding through the dawn. *Well?* he wondered. *What now?*

The trouble with the men on the other rafts in his group had begun late the previous day. An argument had broken out, and somebody on one of the rafts finally pulled a pistol. The fight had centered on whether or not breaking up the group would increase their chances of survival. Somebody had suggested they should strike out separately in the hopes that one of the rafts might sail into a shipping lane.

Mike Kuryla, on the raft next to McCoy, had thought the idea was plain dumb. After the gun appeared, though, he shut up.

McCoy had been in favor of the idea; he was sick of waiting. The water around him had become a floating morgue. Bodies and pieces of bodies were floating by. McCoy had been willing to do almost anything to get away. His raft had been nearly destroyed by the constant pounding of the other rafts as the waves pitched them together.

Suddenly, a plane flew over at what looked to McCoy to be about five thousand feet. The marine pulled out his pistol and this time the gun fired. The plane just kept on flying.

One of the men said, "Give me some of your water."

McCoy was shocked. "I don't have no water," he said. "Hell, you know that."

"You *do* have water. You're keeping it from us!" Now the boy pulled a knife.

"Is that what it's coming to?" said McCoy. "You wanna start killing each other, huh? Fine, but let's use our bare hands." McCoy grabbed the knife away from the boy and tossed it over the raft's side. Then he pitched his pistol as far as he could and said, "All right now, come on. Let's do it."

Nobody moved. What passed for normalcy returned to the raft.

~

TWIBLE'S GROUP

Across the water, in other groups, men were making deals with God. They promised to read the Bible, to write their parents more, to never steal or cheat, so help them, if only they could survive this day.

In the raft group commanded by Ensign Twible, Chief Engineer Redmayne was losing it. He had started sipping salt water sometime late Tuesday night, and he now informed Twible that he was going to swim belowdecks and start the *Indy*'s engines.

Twible was beside himself. Of the original group of 325 sailors, about 200 were still alive. This disorganized mass was operating under the strictest rules of survival of the fittest. Sailors who couldn't muscle onto a raft were doomed to spend every minute floating in their life vests, more fully exposed to the sharks.

And now there was Redmayne to contend with. Twible feared that in his delirium, the wounded officer would drown. For several hours, Twible had been struggling to keep him afloat. He finally jabbed him with a needle fitted with a tube filled with morphine called a Syrette.

Redmayne barked, "Whadya do that for!" and then he slumped over.

The young ensign tied the straps of Redmayne's vest to his own. He would tow the two-hundred-pound officer behind him, like a fish on a stringer.

~

HAYNES'S GROUP

In the early morning light, Dr. Haynes regained consciousness in the arms of the pharmacist's mate John Schmueck. The doctor looked out as far as he could see. But he saw only ocean and more ocean, rolling in ominous green humps over the horizon. Some men had tied hats or socks around their necks, fashioning makeshift protective scarves. They stared at the morning sky with sunken eyes.

Who's there? the eyes seemed to beg as they studied the clouds.

No one, pal, came the answer in their shipmates' hollow faces. *No one but you.*

As the merciless sun rocketed into the sky Wednesday morning, the outlook for rescue was bleak. And yet many of the survivors found themselves reaching even deeper inside and summoning a grim refusal to die. No one believed that help was coming, but they tried to convince one another to hang on.

They had been afloat fifty-five hours. At this point slightly more than half of the nine hundred or so who had left the ship were still alive. Sailors had been dying at an average rate of one every ten minutes for the past three days. And it looked like the cycle would only accelerate.

The seawater was eating Dr. Haynes's sailors alive. Their sunburned, waterlogged arms and legs were stamped with painful red sores, called saltwater ulcers. The salt water was even dissolving hair from some of their bodies. After another cold night in the water, the men's body temperatures hovered around 88 degrees, precariously within the coma zone. Their kidneys were shutting down, their hearts were racing, and they were gasping for air.

And then they began hallucinating en masse. The visions came whirling over the horizon through the bright morning sun. Islands, grocery stores, old girlfriends, wives, automobiles, and mountains of ice cream materialized on the water around the men. They looked on, overjoyed and amazed.

It was the beginning of the final act.

13

HALLUCINATIONS IN FULL BOIL

Morning and afternoon, Wednesday, August 1

~

The rafts of Marine Private McCoy and Captain McVay drifted ahead of what remained of the other groups. McCoy and McVay were about eight miles apart, and each was about seven miles from Haynes.

~

McVAY'S GROUP

Amazingly, Captain McVay's crew was nearly untouched by madness. The other good news was the relative smoothness of the sea, which had replaced Tuesday's swells. Assessing his collection of rafts, McVay knew the sailors were teetering on the brink of exhaustion. He pleaded with the men to stay still and expend as little energy as possible. Quietly, he begged them to keep looking out for planes.

The tension was nearly unbearable. At one point, as many as nine sharks were circling the rafts. The crew had spent hours fishing and they'd had little luck, although sailor John Spinelli had been able to catch one fish. He'd cut it into strips and arranged them on the raft's edge to dry in the sun. But McVay had been afraid to let the boy eat the small, black triangular fish, fearing it might be poisonous. Spinelli obeyed and tossed it overboard. The sight of this was torture for the others, who'd been sucking sullenly on milk tablets or nibbling at their meager rations of salty Spam and crackers.

McVay's four rafts were spread out over seventy-five feet of ocean. He was trying to create as large a visual target as possible for passing aircraft. At 5:00 a.m. he spotted a plane's red and green running lights. Quickly McVay shot two star shells— illuminating rounds—from a pistol he'd scavenged from his raft's emergency box. The plane kept on flying.

John Spinelli didn't like the terrible quiet on the raft, but he was more troubled by what he saw in his captain's eyes. Spinelli knew what McVay must be feeling, but could do nothing. Turning his glance toward another of his raft mates, Spinelli noticed one sailor gazing at an enormous shark trailing their rafts.

The fish had bumped the rafts, nuzzled them, even lifted the rafts' corners as if testing their power. The sailor never took his eyes off the fish. It was like he was hypnotized.

Suddenly, as the shark passed again, the boy slashed out with a tiny, two-inch penknife. Spinelli couldn't believe it— the crazy sailor had actually managed to stab the shark between the eyes!

Cannonballs of water landed around the group of rafts as the shark thrashed, thumping the tiny craft with long, leathery strokes of its tail. It seemed all the rafts would tip and break apart. Some of the men shouted and screamed.

McVay raised his voice: "We are going to be all right! We are going to be all right!"

Like a lid clapped on a box, his firm voice silenced the sailors. They looked at one another, grumbling, and settled back into their corners. Spinelli and some others grabbed their mate with the knife and pinned him to the side of the raft. Someone yanked the knife from his hand and threw it overboard.

McVay knew he had to do something quick if he was to get anyone back to shore. If they didn't kill themselves, they'd starve. He reminded them that rescue had to be on the way. Then he doled out each man's daily ration of one sliver of Spam and a malted milk tablet. He announced that, thenceforth, he would be cutting the rations in half. This would double their survival time, he figured, to twenty days.

As he and his sailors chewed and stared into a blinding

horizon, peace—or something approximating it—gradually returned to the rafts. To while away the long afternoon, McVay started questioning the men about their personal lives. He wanted to know about their wives and girlfriends. He himself fell into a reverie about his comfortable life in D.C. with his wife, Louise.

Spinelli knew that few captains would ever get this personal with their crew, not even in the dire predicament they were in now. He admired McVay's soft-spoken calm. The old man, in his opinion, had been getting the job done—hey, at least they hadn't died yet.

John Spinelli realized he was learning something essential, something he couldn't yet put into words. He and the men listened raptly as the stoic, gray-haired captain confessed, "I'm going to have some explaining to do." McVay didn't know what he might tell the families of the dead—if he survived. He knew there was little he could say that would help.

On board the *Indy*, McVay had sometimes talked of becoming an admiral. But now he said, "I should have gone down with the ship." The sailors on the raft disagreed.

It was as if, in his candor, McVay was discovering what it meant to be a captain and a leader. He had commanded ships, but until the sinking of the *Indy* he'd never felt the full responsibility of the lives he held in his hands. Now he understood what it meant to be placed in harm's way while leading so many young men. He assured the sailors they would be rescued by the next day. And they believed him.

McCOY'S GROUP

In McCoy's raft, sailor Ed Payne had taken to drinking his urine. McCoy was amazed Payne even had anything left to expel. The boy was becoming a real problem, but McCoy didn't blame him. As the afternoon sun pressed down, McCoy was so thirsty he was thinking of drinking his pee himself. But he couldn't bring himself to do it, figuring it might make him even crazier. He reached over the raft and cradled a cool palmful of water. He burned for a sip.

Who am I? Where am I? he wondered.

I'm Giles McCoy from St. Louis, Missouri, and I'm one tough fighter.

McCoy's tongue felt hard and dry, like a root. His skin was cracked and sore, bleeding in places. He thought about his mother and her laugh when she beat him at Ping-Pong. He thought of his father, and the way he'd cried when he brought his son to the train station to head to boot camp.

The young marine reflected on his training. The Marine Corps had taught him how to lie in a stream for hours breathing through a straw, how to shoot to kill, how to *survive*. He'd always had the firm conviction of his own toughness.

Now he realized he hadn't even known what strength really was.

~

HAYNES'S GROUP

In Dr. Haynes's group, the hallucinations were reaching full boil. One boy got in his car and was ready to drive home, but then lost his keys. Another saw an island overflowing with ice-cold coconut milk and dancing girls. One delirious sailor was seen starting an imaginary outboard motor with furious yanks at a rope and then puttering away.

By midafternoon, passenger trains were pounding along imaginary rails ringing the horizon, and hotels were springing up on city blocks floating atop the water. Some of the men checked into the hotels and drowned, while others started swimming to catch the trains and vanished beneath the waves.

At one point, even Dr. Haynes succumbed. Spotting a shark he was seized with the desire to kill it with his bare hands and drink its blood. But no matter how hard he splashed at the creature, no matter how loudly he swore at it, it would not attack. It seemed to be mocking his rage. He couldn't believe it. The shark didn't want to eat him! The doctor paddled away, somehow feeling better.

He then came upon a group of sailors. They looked odd— something was wrong with the picture. They were floating in single file, dog-paddling in place. Haynes asked one of them, "What's up, son?"

"Shhh, Doc," one guy said. "There's a small hotel on the

island there. They got one room and you can get fifteen min-utes' sleep. You get in line—you'll get a turn."

Haynes craned his head and for a moment he believed he could see the hotel wavering atop the water.

Nearby, other odd things were going on. Another twenty-five men had queued up, as if preparing to set out on a journey. They told Haynes matter-of-factly that they were going to swim to Leyte, and that they figured it would take them about two days. They said their goodbyes, promising to meet up again on land. Then they kicked out over the glass of the sea. They made it only two or three hundred yards before sinking.

What struck Haynes as the grandest hallucination of all, how-ever, was the moment when the *Indianapolis* appeared. The ship ghosted over the horizon and sailed back into the sailors' lives.

At times, they yelled that the ship was steaming toward them. At others, it was drifting peacefully below them in the clear, green water, all her flags flying smartly, her portholes relit and gleaming.

Some of the sailors dived down to the ship and began swim-ming through her long passageways, back to their bunks, to the mess halls, and to the water fountains, where they drank deeply. "I found it," they screamed in heartbreaking relief, breaking back to the surface. "There's fresh water aboard! Come on, fellas, let's go! She ain't sunk!"

More men took deep breaths and dived to the ship, and in the aqua light of their dreams they sat at tables eating ice cream and drinking tall glasses of water.

"Don't drink! *Don't do it!*" Haynes shouted, his throat raw, his voice breaking, as he watched their dreams turn to nightmares.

~

McCOY'S GROUP

By late afternoon, the men on McCoy's raft were trying to kill him. At least, he thought they were. Ed Payne swore he was going to jump off the raft. McCoy was certain he wanted to commit suicide. Gray looked like he wanted to jump, too.

Everybody, thought McCoy, was going crazy. Everybody, that is, except Bob Brundige, the nineteen-year-old sailor from Tennessee. He was glad Brundige wasn't losing his grip. He just wished he'd say something.

McCoy shouted at Payne and Gray, "You've got families, relatives—you've got things to live for!"

One of them—Willis Gray—looked up and said, "Live for?"

"We're going through this day after day," said Payne, "and nobody is looking for us. To hell with it! It's easier to die than to live." Payne looked like he really was going to jump.

"Don't you worry, guys," McCoy announced, speaking particularly to Payne. "I'll take care of you. I'll make sure the sharks don't get you."

Payne began moaning, and then he jumped and began to swim. McCoy studied the water; it was so clear, like a glass floor he might walk across. As usual, he could see sharks down there, circling. He dived and started swimming after Payne.

He swam about fifty feet and caught the sailor. Grabbing hold of his vest, he dragged the blubbering sailor back to the raft. He yelled up to Brundige, "Come on, give me a damn hand here!" And Brundige, tall and strong, reached down and lifted Payne into the raft.

McCoy swam up through the hole in the busted bow. He pulled himself onto the suspended lattice floor. And then Payne got up on the side of the raft, looked around, and jumped over again.

McCoy looked at Brundige, thinking, *I saved him once, do I gotta do it again?* He looked at the sharks and jumped. He swam out over them and stroked up behind Payne, jerked him hard, and brought him back to the raft.

Now McCoy was mad—and dead tired. It was as if all the blood had drained from his arms and legs. He was so thirsty it was a struggle not to sip some salt water as he splashed back aboard. He slammed Payne against the rail of the raft. Payne was crying, and McCoy looked at him and whacked him on the face, screaming, "Now, dammit, cut that out, cuz you're going to kill yourself!"

Payne's eyes widened, and his head rolled back and forth on the rail. "Why'd you hit me?" he asked. "Don't hit me no more!" He was crying, but no tears were coming; Payne was too dehydrated for tears.

McCoy turned around, and there was Willis Gray on the raft's edge, jumping. This time, McCoy just sat there and watched. He thought Gray was dumb for jumping. He said it out loud: "You know, you are a real turd."

"Hell, we just can't leave him out there," announced Brundige.

McCoy looked at him. "I just don't have no more fire." Then Brundige hit the water. Batting and kicking at the sharks, he towed the boy back to the raft.

Utter hopelessness swept over McCoy. "You know what?" he said to Brundige. "They're not comin'. Nobody's going to rescue us." He turned to the rest of them: "We are going to die," he said. "We are all going to die."

It felt good to say it. His stomach felt queasy, as if he had butterflies. In fact, all day he'd felt nauseated. And it wasn't from swallowing fuel oil. It was a sickness that came from lying to himself that he'd survive.

"We are going to die," he said again.

14

FATHER CONWAY AND
CAPTAIN PARKE

Afternoon and evening, Wednesday, August 1

HAYNES'S GROUP

The sun was like a hammer in the sky. As the day wore on, the bodies piled on the surface of the sea in ragged heaps that swirled as the sharks tugged them from below.

Dr. Haynes set out to bury the newly dead. He was no longer a doctor, it seemed; he was now a coroner. So be it. The realization wrenched him back to reality, but this was a blessing he had mixed feelings about.

As he paddled by, some of the sailors stirred, lifting their oil-caked heads to stare bleary-eyed at the sun. "Hey, Doc, take a look at this guy, will ya!" a few of the more lucid called out. "Hey, Doc, is this guy alive?"

Stroking up to one boy, Haynes gently lifted him by the hair and peered into his eyes. "Are you alive, son?" he asked.

"Yes, Doctor, I'm alive," the man croaked.

"Good. That's real good." He moved on to the next candidate.

"Son?" He lifted the head. "Are you with us?" There was no reply. "Son?" Haynes tapped on the cold, opened eyeball. When he found a reflex, he felt an immense sense of relief.

Then he moved quickly to the next boy. He tapped again; the boy's eyes were bloodshot and swollen. Haynes knew it was a sign the sailor had ingested too much salt water. There was no reflex. It was like touching the blank and glassy eye of a stuffed animal. Haynes had to declare the boy dead.

"This man is dead," he said aloud. It was strange, but saying it made it seem more real. It made him feel like he wasn't alone. At the sound of Haynes's voice, several men turned to watch. More than a few of them didn't have life vests. They were half dog-paddling and half drowning, heroically supported by comrades who themselves were close to giving up.

The men supporting these swimmers had enormous sores on their hips from the chafing of their heavy loads. Yet none of them wanted to let go of their charges. They were clinging to them as if saving themselves. The sailors without vests had either untied them in their delirium or had voluntarily taken them off because they were losing buoyancy. Either way, they needed relief.

Time was critical—Haynes needed the dead boy's life vest—and he moved quickly. It was not easy work because his burned hands were badly swollen, practically unusable. He tried not to look into the boy's eyes as he struggled to loosen the knotted straps. They were soaked with fuel oil, which made them impossibly tight. Untying them was painful, methodical work.

When he was done, he removed the boy's dog tags. He wrapped them around his own arm, where they clinked tinnily. Haynes then paddled behind the body. He placed one hand on the vest's collar, and gave a gentle pull, easing out first the shoulders and then the arms. It looked very much like someone removing a coat from a sleeping child. Finally, the corpse slid free from the vest.

Haynes quickly tossed the vest aside and then snatched the body before it could sink. The bodies of the bigger men required more strength than those of the smaller ones, and strength was something Haynes didn't have much of. Still, he was determined not to let any corpse sink without praying over it.

He drew the cold, wet body close, grabbed it tight in a bear hug, and paused. Aboard a ship, the chaplain would do this duty, but Father Conway was close to death himself. Haynes groped for a way to say goodbye to these sailors, many of whom he knew only in passing. But he always said something. With his cheek pressed to the dead boy's cheek, he could smell the salt and sweat. Then he began: *Our Father, who art in heaven, hallowed be thy name . . . Thy kingdom come, thy will be done . . .*

Sometimes he made it to the end of the Lord's Prayer, and

sometimes he didn't. After several hours of burying the dead, he was often so spent that he could do nothing more than hold the dead boy and pray in silence.

He opened his arms and watched the body fall. It dropped for a long time, twirling feet first, like a man falling down a crystalline elevator shaft.

Why, oh why, Haynes wondered, *can't I do anything to save these men?*

~

McCOY'S GROUP

McCoy's despair was so deep he felt he was going to die within the next hour. He decided it might as well happen now. It made no sense, he knew, but nothing did now. Dying suddenly seemed like play. He untied his vest, tossed it into the raft, and then slipped over the side.

Brundige boomed, "What the hell you doing, Marine?"

McCoy ignored him. The water was cool, the air hot, the shock instant. McCoy stroked around the raft. To his surprise, he was having fun. Looking down, he could see thirty or forty feet below. He wondered what the water felt like down there where the sharks circled in glassy coils.

McCoy dived. He felt like he was flying, as his head poked through a cool band of water. Half his body was warm, the other cold. He looked up and to his surprise he saw that he was only about six feet deep.

He prayed that his mother would understand why he had not been able to make it home; he prayed that she would know he'd tried his hardest to get there.

Finally the marine broke the surface, paddled over to the raft, and hoisted himself up. And then he began scrubbing himself with his T-shirt, rubbing at the smeared oil on his chest and arms. He wanted to be clean because he wanted to be identified if anybody found his body. He realized he'd probably be chewed up by sharks, but he hoped they'd at least leave his face. He wanted somebody to be able to recognize him.

Brundige told him, "You still got oil all over you, you know. You stupid thing." He said it again: "You stupid thing."

McCoy liked that—*You stupid thing*. It made him laugh. He *was* a stupid thing. Sitting in this ocean, he felt like nothing more than a speck. All his life, he had thought he was tough. Now he felt like a speck, and he felt relieved to know the truth. He looked at Payne, Outland, and Gray, who were now passed out, bobbing in the water up to their chins. McCoy decided he had better tie them together for safekeeping. He asked Brundige to help, and they drew the sailors so close that their foreheads were touching.

McCoy and Brundige cinched up all the straps on the vests to prevent the three sailors' heads from falling into the water. They floated like that inside the raft, their feet dangling. McCoy and Brundige were each in a corner, hanging on the rails.

Sometime before nightfall, they started betting each other

about who was going to die first. "I'm sure gonna stay alive longer than you," McCoy said.

"Like hell," Brundige shot back. "I'm a Tennessee farmer, and I'm pretty damn tough."

"Well, I'm a marine from Missourah, and I'm a lot tougher."

"You go to hell." After a while, they fell silent and drifted. Around them, Payne, Outland, and Gray started moaning. The sharks were circling the raft again.

"Well," said Brundige, "I guess nobody's gonna miss me but my mom and dad."

"My mother's gonna miss me," said McCoy. "And I'm sure my dad will, too. And I also know I'm gonna outlive you."

"We'll see."

"You know," McCoy said finally, "if some damn shark gets me, I hope it gets indigestion." He laughed. "I really hope he has a hard time *digesting* me."

They fell asleep with their heads resting on each other's shoulders.

~

HAYNES'S GROUP

By nightfall, Haynes was burying Father Conway and Captain Parke. The big marine went first. His selfless lending of life vests to struggling swimmers had finally taken its toll. Parke, an astonishingly strong and disciplined man, had died in mid-hallucination;

he suddenly broke away from the group and started swimming for the horizon. His death shocked those still lucid enough to understand it.

Conway was next. The deteriorating condition of the priest crushed Haynes.

For the past three days, Conway had kept drowning men afloat. He prayed with them as they died, refusing to quit even when it must have felt impossible to swim another inch. A few hours ago, however, he had finally succumbed to delirium, singing in Latin and babbling prayers. As Conway sang, Haynes had cradled the naked priest in his arms, smoothing his balding, sunburned head with a gentle hand.

Conway's condition worsened and his keening grew in intensity. Soon he was blessing Haynes, hitting him repeatedly in the face. Haynes did nothing to stop the crazed priest. He watched and waited for him to die.

When Conway fell limp, the silence was deafening. Haynes heard only the water gurgle and swish around him. When it was clear that Conway was dead, Haynes removed his vest and set his friend's body sailing into the deep.

Haynes was left holding the dog tags he'd collected from the sailors he'd personally buried over the past three days. There were well over one hundred, their silver chains wrapped tightly around his fist. Suddenly they felt so heavy he could hardly believe it. He was so exhausted he could barely lift them up anymore. Reluctantly he tossed them away.

~

Back on Leyte, the port director's office noted once again that the *Indianapolis* had failed to arrive. Once again, she was dutifully marked as overdue. The thinking in the office was that she would reach the harbor the next day, Thursday, August 2.

On the island of Tinian, B-29s were taking off continually, loaded with thousands of pounds of bombs. During the raids, a new plane lifted off every few seconds. The sky over Japan was raining bombs.

In an air-conditioned bunker on Tinian, a team of weapons specialists had gathered. They were huddled in the specially built bunker to assemble the pieces of the atomic bomb code-named "Little Boy." Around this same time, the flight crews of the 509th Composite Group, led by Lieutenant Colonel Paul Tibbets, were practicing secret dummy bombing runs over Japan. Tibbets would eventually drop Little Boy from his B-29 *Enola Gay* on Hiroshima.

Nobody thought to miss McVay and his sailors.

PART III

15

PELELIU ISLAND AND
HOPE FROM ABOVE

Thursday, August 2, 1945

Something had gone wrong with the navigation antenna again. Lieutenant Chuck Gwinn wondered if he should land the bomber and fix it before getting airborne again. Or should he push ahead on his patrol sector, hoping for the best as he navigated by the seat of his pants? Gwinn decided to land. Better safe than sorry.

He banked the bomber back over the jungle scrub of Peleliu and brought the big plane down. A rancher's son from San Martin, California, Gwinn was in his third year of service in the navy. With him this morning was a crew of four naval aviators.

Gwinn, twenty-four, had logged over 1,000 flight hours as a

navy test pilot. Today, Thursday, August 2, he and his crew were flying a PV-1 bomber, call-named *Gambler 17*. The bomber, with a split rear tail and two engines, had a range of 950 miles. On board, she carried two forward-firing .50-caliber machine guns and six .30-caliber guns on flex mounts. Her bomb bay could hold 2,500 pounds of bombs.

Chuck Gwinn's job was to search out and bomb Japanese submarines. Although he had patrolled miles and miles of the Pacific between Peleliu Island and the Japanese homeland, he and his flyboys still had not seen any action. Nothing.

Life on Peleliu was miserable. The island was a no-man's-land, 500 miles from the coast of the Philippines, and 500 miles north of New Guinea. Daily temperatures reached 120 degrees, and stayed there. The humidity was drenching. The island had been the scene of one of the last major battles before the U.S. Marines' decisive victories at Iwo Jima and then Okinawa. The Battle of Peleliu had come at a great cost: about 10,000 marine casualties. But the entire garrison of 10,500 entrenched Japanese soldiers had been wiped out. A bloodbath.

Now the island was home to the Peleliu unit of the search and reconnaissance command, which fell under the supervision of Vice Admiral George Murray, commander of Marianas naval operations back in Guam. This was the same command from which the *Indy* had sailed six days earlier and McVay had received his sailing orders. Reporting to Vice Admiral Murray was Captain Oliver Naquin, a surface operations officer. Naquin was the officer who had neglected to tell McVay about Japanese subs along the Peddie route, part of which Gwinn would soon be patrolling.

At this morning's flight briefing, Gwinn had learned that he might see American convoys passing in his patrol sector, which ran north from Peleliu for five hundred miles. Other than that, the coast should be clear. He was to keep his eyes peeled for enemy subs cruising, and to sink any he spotted with a dive-bombing run.

Gwinn's other task was to test out a new antenna used in navigation. The long whip antenna was attached to the rear flank of the plane and steadied with a weighted sock, which kept it from slipping around. The problem was, the sock wouldn't stay on.

By 9:00 a.m., Gwinn had a new one secured, and forty-five minutes after his original departure, he taxied down the runway and roared the bomber north, over the Philippine Sea.

~

Seven hundred miles to the west of Gwinn, on the island of Leyte, Lieutenant William A. Green received a report of the nonarrival of the USS *Indianapolis* from the naval operating base. Green's job in the office of the Philippine Sea Frontier was to monitor incoming dispatches regarding shipping traffic. In the case of emergency, he was to take up the matter with his superior, Captain Alfred Granum, the operations officer who maintained the office's plotting board. It was Granum who had registered the *Indianapolis* as "arrived" in Leyte two days earlier.

This was the second nonarrival report Green had received; a similar report had come in on Wednesday. Now he requested permission from the plotting section to remove the ship entirely from the plotting board. Once more, it was simply assumed that the *Indy* had been diverted to other action.

~

Gwinn leveled the PV-1 off at three thousand feet, the prescribed altitude for patrol and recon. The sea below him blinked like shattered stained glass. Scanning the horizon, he saw nothing.

And then, the new sock on the whip antenna fell off. This time, Gwinn kept flying. He would make do, although his radioman informed him that long-range communications would be rendered inoperative.

The antenna was whipping back and forth against the aluminum side of the plane. At 11:00 a.m., Gwinn decided to try to fix it by jerry-rigging some kind of new weight. He didn't know exactly what he was doing; he was making this up as he went along. The plane's bombardier stood aft, looking out a window, trying to figure out what they could do to keep the antenna from beating the plane up any further. Inching out of his pilot's seat in the cramped cockpit, Gwinn made his way down the narrow passage of the plane toward the rear, ready to give the bombardier a hand. Through the window in the PV-1's floor, he gazed at the endless miles of blue sea.

And then he spotted something. It looked like an oil slick.

It probably meant there was a Japanese submarine nearby, perhaps disabled by an earlier attack. If an American ship had been downed, Gwinn reasoned, he would have read about it in a report.

He knelt down on the cold floor of the plane, the engines thundering in his ears. Could it be true? Would they see action? He jumped up and headed back to the cockpit. It sure looked like the slick of a leaking sub. Gwinn was ecstatic.

He changed the course of the plane and followed the slick to the north, beginning preparations for a bombing run. The bomb bay doors opened and he ordered the bombs, snug in racks and hanging ready to be "pickled," or dropped.

Gwinn next ordered the depth charges readied. The charges looked like fifty-five-gallon drums and were loaded with the explosive Torpex. They could be preset to detonate at different depths and then dropped out the bomb bay doors.

At 11:20 a.m., Gwinn lowered the PV-1 and started cruising at two hundred miles per hour up the oil slick. Over the intercom, he told his bombardier to get ready. After flying about five miles, cruising at nine hundred feet, he spotted something in the water.

But what was it? Gwinn was confused. As it came into focus, he realized it was a group of figures, and they seemed to be waving—it looked like they were slapping at the water, as if trying to attract attention. Enemy? Friendly? He had to think fast.

He yelled over the intercom to abort the bombing run and banked for another pass.

Gwinn took the plane down to three hundred feet and roared up the slick. He quickly counted about thirty heads. He took a dead reckoning fix (estimation using direction and distance traveled) because the navigation antenna was inoperable—he needed some kind of location to report what he was finding.

A patrol plane, Gwinn's PV-1 was loaded with emergency life rafts, beakers of water, life vests, and other lifesaving gear. As the plane passed low, Gwinn's crew dropped a raft, vests, and a sonobuoy out the rear side hatch. The sonobuoy was a one-way floating microphone used in anti-submarine warfare. Aiming the falling equipment was tricky—he feared hitting the floating bodies. The blackened shapes were now waving frantically as he passed over. He couldn't see their faces clearly—it looked like they were covered with . . . oil? As he flew, he saw others who were clinging to life rafts.

Gwinn hoped that whoever it was he'd spotted would swim over to the sonobuoy and yell out a name, an identity—anything. So far, no sound was coming back.

In an instant, his mission had flipped from search and destroy to search and rescue. At 11:25 a.m., he radioed a message to the search and reconnaissance headquarters on Peleliu; it read: SIGHTED 30 SURVIVORS 011–30 NORTH 133–30 EAST— the numbers indicating the latitude and longitude of the sighting.

This was the first report of the USS *Indianapolis* disaster.

But who were these people in the water? The idea that they were U.S. men seemed out of the question. Gwinn was certain that he would have been briefed if an American ship had been sunk. He counted close to seventy more heads, and then after another minute, spotted at least fifty more. The numbers indicated that these weren't survivors from a sub, which carried crews of one hundred or less. These sailors had to have come from a major ship.

Gwinn wagged his wings—*I see you*—and skimmed low overhead, now looking down at bodies so closely crowded around the rafts that it was hard to estimate their number. He could make out lone swimmers only if they kicked the water and raised a splash. When they stopped kicking, they melted into the blue of the sea, as if swallowed by it.

The pilot, whose vision was somewhat occluded, could ultimately make out four loosely scattered groups. The first contained about thirty people and was approximately six miles from the second group of about forty; the third group, two miles from the second, looked like about fifty-five to seventy-five people. There was also, Gwinn now saw, a fourth group, which numbered around twenty-five to thirty-five.

Gwinn, in fact, had just spotted parts of both Dr. Haynes's group of swimmers and the large raft group under the command of Ensign Harlan Twible. Over the course of the night, both groups had been slowly breaking up into scattered clusters. Gwinn just missed Captain McVay and his small band of nine men and four rafts. Nor did he see McCoy and his gang of four. These two groups had drifted about eight miles ahead of the Haynes and Twible groups.

In the last fourteen hours, McCoy had drifted some

twenty-three miles, for an astonishing total of about one hundred and five miles since the sinking three days earlier. McVay had drifted another sixteen miles in the same period for a total of one hundred and three. Haynes and Twible had each covered about seventeen miles and drifted roughly ninety-seven and eighty-seven miles, respectively, in all.

As Gwinn circled, they continued their swift momentum, driven by the current and the wind.

A VISUAL
EXPLORATION OF
THE USS *INDIANAPOLIS*

One year after its commissioning, the USS *Indianapolis* leaves the Philadelphia navy yard, June 1933. [AP/Wide World Photos]

On his way back from South America in 1936, President Franklin D. Roosevelt participates in his ship of state's equator-crossing festivities. Here, he appears before King Neptune's Court, made up of *Indianapolis* crew members. [AP/Wide World Photos]

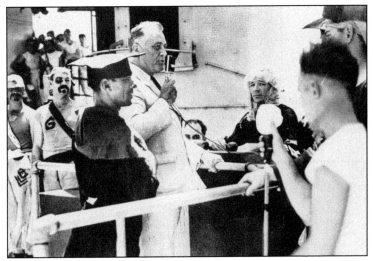

A burial at sea aboard the *Indianapolis*, August 1942. Tipped into the sea following a twenty-one-gun salute, the body was weighted by a forty-pound ammunition shell; the draped flag was later sent home to the man's family. [National Archives]

Admiral Raymond Spruance (front row, fifth from left) with his staff aboard the *Indianapolis*, circa 1945. Widely regarded as one of the navy's most brilliant military planners, Spruance commanded the Fifth Fleet from the *Indianapolis*. [Naval Historical Center]

Admiral Ernest King (center) visits the Marianas Islands on board the *Indianapolis*, July 18, 1944, with Admiral Chester W. Nimitz (left) and Admiral Spruance. [Naval Historical Center]

Indianapolis officers on deck in 1945 (front row, left to right): Cmdr. Johns Janney, navigator; Captain Charles McVay; Cmdr. Joseph Flynn, executive officer; Cmdr. Glen DeGrave, engineering officer; (back row, left to right): unknown; Lt. Cmdr. K. C. Moore, first lieutenant; Lt. Cmdr. Lewis Haynes, medical officer; Lt. Cmdr. Earl O'Dell Henry, dental officer; Lt. Cmdr. Charles Hayes. DeGrave was put ashore at Pearl Harbor prior to the sinking; of the rest of the group, only McVay and Haynes survived. [Courtesy of the collections of Bill Van Daalen and Lewis Haynes]

ABOVE LEFT: Dr. Lewis Haynes, pictured before his tenure aboard the USS *Indianapolis*, circa 1942. At one point in the war, Haynes went thirty-nine months without leave. [Courtesy of the collection of Dr. Lewis Haynes]

ABOVE RIGHT: Marine corps captain Edward L. Parke stands at attention on the *Indianapolis* quarterdeck as Captain McVay presents him with a Silver Star, awarded for bravery during the battle for Saipan in 1944. [Courtesy of the collection of Giles McCoy]

Commodore Norman Gillette, acting commander for the Philippine Sea Frontier at Leyte, in 1944, ten months before the *Indianapolis* was sunk. Both he and his subordinate Alfred Granum fought the letters of reprimand they received from naval command after McVay's court martial. [AP/Wide World Photos]

Commodore Jacob H. Jacobson, commandant, Naval Operating Base at Leyte, did not deem it his responsibility to monitor the arrival of the *Indianapolis* at Leyte, and his officers took no action when the ship was discovered to be overdue in port. Jacobson was not reprimanded for his decision, but his subordinates Lt. Cmdr. Sancho and Lt. Gibson were. [National Archives]

Captain Oliver Naquin, Surface Operations Officer, was privy to enemy Japanese submarine activity on the Peddie/Leyte route, as well as the sinking of the USS *Underhill*, yet he failed to warn McVay of possible danger. Although cited in the navy inspector general report, Naquin was not censured in the aftermath of the sinking. [AP/Wide World Photos]

July 10, 1945: The USS *Indianapolis* at Mare Island, California, shortly before her final voyage. The ship would be sunk nearly three weeks later after delivering to Tinian Island the components of "Little Boy," the atom bomb that would be dropped on Hiroshima. [Courtesy of the collection of Giles McCoy]

The I-58 was part of the Tamon group, the largest and most technologically advanced of Japan's submarines. By mid-1945, however, they were not considered a significant threat, which may have led to a false sense of security within U.S. Naval Command and to the July 30 torpedoing of the *Indianapolis*. [Naval Historical Center]

The crew of the PV-1 Ventura bomber who accidentally discovered the crew of the *Indianapolis* during a routine patrol on August 2, 1945. As pilot Wilbur "Chuck" Gwinn circled, he could see crew members drowning in sodden life vests. Front row, left to right: Lt. Wilbur Gwinn and Lt. Warren Colwell; back row, left to right: Herbert Hickman, William Hartman, and Joseph Johnson. [Courtesy of the collection of Robert Krauss]

Pilot Adrian Marks (front row, second from right), who landed the plane in dangerous ocean swells and picked up fifty-six survivors, and his crew of the PBY *Catalina*. [Courtesy of the collection of Giles McCoy]

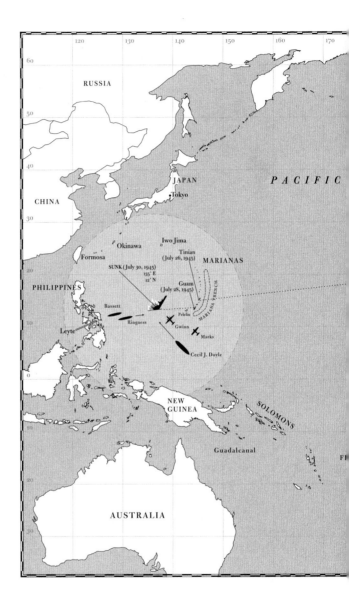

RUSSIA

PACIFIC

JAPAN

•Tokyo

CHINA

Okinawa   Iwo Jima
                 Tinian
Formosa   (July 26, 1945)   MARIANAS

        SUNK (July 30, 1945)
                  135° E
                  12° N   Guam
                               (July 28, 1945)

PHILIPPINES   Peleliu

        Bassett
                                MARIANA TRENCH
        Ringness
                        Gwinn
Leyte
                          Marks

                  Cecil J. Doyle

                NEW
                GUINEA   SOLOMONS

                        Guadalcanal

        AUSTRALIA

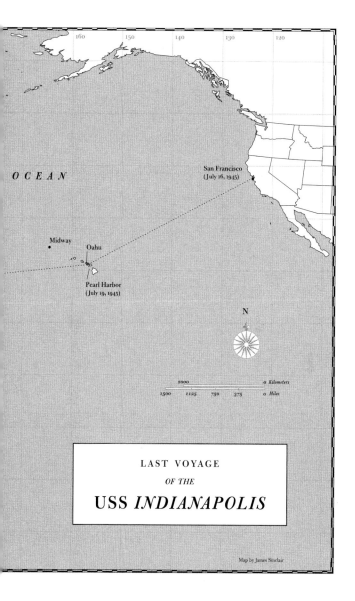

160   150   140   130   120

O C E A N

San Francisco
(July 16, 1945)

Midway

Oahu

Pearl Harbor
(July 19, 1945)

N

2000   0 *Kilometers*
1500   1125   750   375   0 *Miles*

LAST VOYAGE

OF THE

USS *INDIANAPOLIS*

Map by James Sinclair

Two survivors (William R. Mulvey on left) aboard a raft pull themselves toward the rescue ship *Register*, after four and a half days afloat, sunburned, dehydrated, and severely malnourished. Most survivors also suffered massive skin ulcers. [National Archives]

Mike Kuryla (left), Bob McGuiggan (center), and an unidentified sailor in the hospital on Peleliu. High school friends from Chicago, Kuryla and McGuiggan each thought the other had died before being reunited. [Courtesy of the collections of Bob McGuiggan and Mike Kuryla]

Exhausted survivors (William R. Mulvey on right), awaiting transfer to the hospital ship USS *Tranquility*, rest on a barge at Peleliu. [Courtesy of the collection of Giles McCoy]

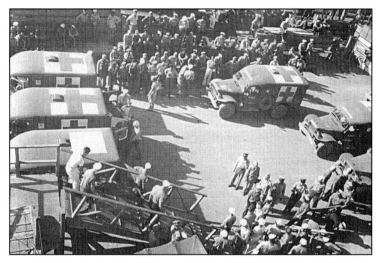

Welcomed by sailors and nurses on Guam, the survivors
are transferred from the USS *Tranquility* to ambulances
destined for local hospitals. [U.S. Naval Historical Center]

August 1945: Admiral Spruance, visiting the survivors at Base 18
Hospital in Guam, awards them Purple Hearts. [National Archives]

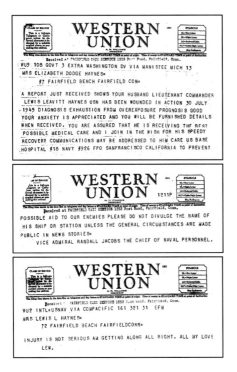

WU9 108 GOVT 3 EXTRA WASHINGTON DV VIA MANISTEE MICH 13
MRS ELIZABETH DODGE HAYNES=
    57 FAIRFIELD BEACH FAIRFIELD CONN=

A REPORT JUST RECEIVED SHOWS YOUR HUSBAND LIEUTENANT COMMANDER
LEWIS LEAVITT HAYNES USN HAS BEEN WOUNDED IN ACTION 30 JULY
1945 DIAGNOSIS EXHAUSTION FROM OVEREXPOSURE PROGNOSIS GOOD
YOUR ANXIETY IS APPRECIATED AND YOU WILL BE FURNISHED DETAILS
WHEN RECEIVED. YOU ARE ASSURED THAT HE IS RECEIVING THE BEST
POSSIBLE MEDICAL CARE AND I JOIN IN THE WISH FOR HIS SPEEDY
RECOVERY COMMUNICATIONS MAY BE ADDRESSED TO HIM CARE US BASE
HOSPITAL #18 NAVY #926 FPO SANFRANCISCO CALIFORNIA TO PREVENT

The telegrams Elizabeth Haynes received from Washington and from her husband, Lewis, apprising her of his condition. [Courtesy of the collection of Lewis Haynes]

POSSIBLE AID TO OUR ENEMIES PLEASE DO NOT DIVULGE THE NAME OF
HIS SHIP OR STATION UNLESS THE GENERAL CIRCUMSTANCES ARE MADE
PUBLIC IN NEWS STORIES=
    VICE ADMIRAL RANDALL JACOBS THE CHIEF OF NAVAL PERSONNEL.

WU2 INTL=USNAV VIA COMPACIFIC 161 321 31 EFM
MRS LEWIS L HAYNES=
    72 FAIRFIELD BEACH FAIRFIELDCONN=

INJURY IS NOT SERIOUS AM GETTING ALONG ALL RIGHT. ALL MY LOVE
    LEW.

Marine privates first class Paul Uffelman (left), Giles McCoy (center), and Mel Jacob (right), sailing for the United States aboard the USS *Hollandia*, after their convalescence on Guam. Of the thirty-nine-man marine detachment aboard the *Indianapolis*, only nine survived the disaster. [Courtesy of the collections of Bill Van Daalen and Giles McCoy]

The announcement of the sinking in the *New York Times*, which appeared August 15, 1945, was overshadowed by the day's bigger headline news.

The survivors of the USS *Indianapolis* sail home aboard the USS *Hollandia*. [Courtesy of the collection of Giles McCoy]

Captain McVay, testifying at the Washington navy yard, December 1945. McVay was the first captain in the history of the U.S. Navy to be court-martialed subsequent to losing his ship in an act of war. [Courtesy of the collection of Giles McCoy]

Testifying at the court-martial on December 5, 1945, Dr. Haynes told the court that "under McVay's command the *Indianapolis* was a very efficient, trim fighting ship, and I would be honored and pleased to serve under him again." [AP/Wide World Photos]

Commander Mochitsura Hashimoto, of the Japanese submarine I-58, arrives in Washington, D.C., on December 10, 1945. The highly unusual prosecution's move of calling a former military enemy to testify raised protests in Congress and in newspapers across the country. [AP/Wide World Photos]

Former marine private McCoy greets Rear Admiral McVay at the Indianapolis airport during the first survivors' reunion in July 1960. The two men had not seen each other since the court-martial. [Courtesy of the collection of Giles McCoy]

Fifteen years after the sinking, McCoy, David P. Kemp, Jr., Felton Outland, and Ed Payne (left to right) are reunited in Indianapolis. McCoy and his raft mates were the last survivors to be pulled from the water. [Courtesy of the collection of Giles McCoy]

16

SUPPLIES FALLING FROM THE SKY

Afternoon, Thursday, August 2

HAYNES'S GROUP

Dr. Haynes had drifted into another world, far from the realization of what was happening. When he looked up to find life vests tumbling out of the sky, it seemed to him the heavens were raining gear. When he saw them crash about one hundred feet away, he felt too weak to swim to them. But he tried.

With painfully slow strokes, his neck bleeding as his own waterlogged vest chafed against it, he somehow managed to cover the distance. He grabbed a few vests, hugged them tight, and then steeled himself for the return trip to his men.

Minute by minute, he felt his mind clearing as the glinting

plane circled. He counted about one hundred men left in his scattered group, which had numbered at least four hundred three days earlier. At this point, because of the failing vests, each boy was sunk up to his chin. They treaded furiously just to keep their noses above the water. Even as the PV-1 circled overhead, some sailors gave up and drowned.

Bob Gause waved his hat as if it were a signal flag. Never much of a churchgoer, he'd nonetheless spent the last twenty-four hours praying with all his heart. It seemed it had paid off. All around him, men started singing out of tune. Others became so excited they started flapping their arms, often drowning themselves in the process.

Jack Cassidy, covered with saltwater ulcers, was wearing three life vests, but he was still sinking into the heaving sea. His eyes were so matted with fuel oil that he had to pry them open with bleeding fingers. He managed to look up and see the plane, and the dye bombs that were now being released from its belly.

As the orange dye spread around them and marked the sailors' positions, some of them began to sing even louder. They shouted that the plane was an angel. They truly believed saviors were visiting from heaven.

Dr. Haynes, however, noticed with alarm that in the commotion his dwindling group was continuing to drift apart. Operating on nothing but a vapor of adrenaline, he tore open the pockets of the new life vests. He was looking for the precious cans of water he guessed would be stored there. But every one of the cans had exploded on impact when they hit the ocean.

The survivors, Haynes knew, might live only a few more hours without water. He watched anxiously as some of the men made their way to the rubber life raft that the plane had dropped. Soon the raft was crammed with as many as twenty men, with another twenty or so clinging desperately to the lifelines.

Meanwhile, Gwinn was trying to get a proper navigation fix, which would offer a more accurate position than the estimated location he had given. He struggled to the back of the plane, grabbed hold of the antenna wire, and reeled it in. Then he fitted it with a piece of rubber hose, hoping that its weight would be enough to prevent the antenna from tearing loose.

The radioman announced that he had, in fact, just gotten a reading. Now Gwinn had a position to report. He was in business. He then sent a second message. More urgent than the first he had sent an hour and twenty minutes earlier, it read: SEND RESCUE SHIP 11–54 N 133–47 E 150 SURVIVORS IN LIFEBOAT AND JACKETS.

With this new message, the otherwise normal day back at the Peleliu search and recon command suddenly unraveled. The chaos quickly spread throughout the Philippine Sea Frontier, and finally to the command in Guam.

The search and recon unit had already responded to the first message. Lieutenant Commander George Atteberry, Gwinn's superior officer, jumped into action. At 12:05 p.m., when Atteberry had received Gwinn's message, he thought his pilot had stumbled upon the survivors of a plane wreck. He knew he had to act quickly.

Worried for Gwinn's safety, Atteberry quickly calculated that the pilot had enough fuel for another four hours of flight. Atteberry wanted to make sure, therefore, that the survivors were covered by some kind of air support after Gwinn's departure.

And so he decisively took matters into his own hands. He called across the island to the duty station handling the dispatch of a squadron of amphibious planes called PBY-5As. These planes were designed with floats to land on water, and their crews specialized in locating survivors of ship and air disasters.

Atteberry informed the duty officer that he wanted a PBY to leave immediately in order to relieve Gwinn by 3:30 p.m. But the duty officer wanted official confirmation of the spotting of survivors.

Unfortunately, there was none. No commanding officers above Atteberry's rank knew about the accident yet. Events had unfolded so quickly that Atteberry had not had time to transmit a message to his superiors.

Frustrated, Atteberry hung up and decided to drive over to the duty station and hash it out in person. Once there, however, he realized that the duty officer would never be able to get a Catalina rescue plane up in time to meet Gwinn's turnaround time. He quickly drove back to his office and ordered up a Ventura bomber from his own squadron. The plane was fueled, and Atteberry and a crew of four lifted off the island.

The time was 12:44 p.m.

A minute later, Gwinn's second, more urgent message requesting that a rescue ship be dispatched to his search area arrived at Atteberry's command on Peleliu. Because he was in the air, Atteberry did not intercept this transmission, but he would be arriving at the rescue scene in an hour and a half.

Other officers did receive it, however, and immediately swung the effort into hyperdrive. One of the largest sea rescues in the history of the U. S. Navy was underway.

Vice Admiral Murray on Guam was one of the people who got the message. Less than fifteen minutes later, he sent a dispatch to the command on the western Carolines—the island chain to which Peleliu belonged—that read: ORDER 2 DESTROYERS AT BEST SPEED . . . RESCUE 150 SURVIVORS IN LIFEBOATS.

As the rescue effort heated up on Guam, a navy PBM-5, an amphibious transport plane, was flying patrol near the *Indy* sailors in the water. The flight crew noticed a brilliant flash, as if reflected off a large bronze mirror. Looking down, they saw a large oil slick glinting below them. Radar reported another plane in the area, which they determined was friendly. It was, in fact, Gwinn and his crew.

The PBM-5 emerged from the clouds, and the crew began dropping all of their survival gear, including their own life jackets and rafts. They reported large and small groups with sharks all around the perimeter. When they had nothing left to drop, they regained altitude. The pilot radioed Leyte requesting permission to put down and pick up survivors. The request was denied.

~

Lieutenant Commander George Atteberry, in his Ventura bomber, call-named *Gambler Leader*, arrived at the wreckage site at 2:15 p.m. Gwinn, who had been circling the scene, led Atteberry on a half-hour tour of the area. Now they had to wait for a ship to pick up the men. They hoped they were reassuring the sailors in the water by continuing to circle overhead.

By this point, Gwinn was definitely running out of fuel. Atteberry was forced to send him back to Peleliu. Gwinn, who had spent an emotional four hours flying over the frantic sailors in the water, was shaky and worried as he headed back to his base.

Atteberry had patrolled the area alone for a half hour when, to his surprise, the call numbers of another plane came over the radio. The plane belonged to Lieutenant Adrian Marks. He was a tall, slim, twenty-eight-year-old lawyer from Indiana who had been a navy flier and instructor for three years.

Marks was part of the Catalina squadron that Atteberry had tried to raise two hours earlier back in Peleliu. He had been hunkered down in a sweltering Quonset hut, trying to decipher what appeared to be a garbled radio message. It read, in part: "Am circling life rafts." It was from Gwinn, and upon reading it, Marks had jumped into action. He thought maybe a carrier pilot had been forced to ditch in the open sea.

Marks went immediately to the Catalinas' HQ. He had just missed Atteberry but found out that he had been looking for a plane. Marks knew that the standby plane was already out on a mission. If he left, there would be no planes available to be dispatched in case of an emergency. He weighed the decision, decided this *was* an emergency, and fueled up his plane, the *Playmate 2*.

Marks's crew consisted of nine aviators, including one co-pilot, two radiomen, and two bombardiers responsible for dropping bombs. The mammoth plane was loaded with life rafts, parachute flares, dye markers, and shipwreck kits containing water and rations. Bigger than Atteberry's Ventura bomber, the PBY-5A Catalina, nicknamed "Dumbo," was a two-engine, high-wing plane built for hunting subs. It could also land in smooth water to pick up downed pilots. Landing in the rolling open ocean would be dicey, to say the least.

At 12:42 p.m., Marks had taken off from Peleliu. He followed the coordinates Gwinn had radioed from the wreckage sight. During the three-hour, 280-mile flight, a call came over his radio from one of the ships, a destroyer escort named the USS *Cecil J. Doyle*. Its captain, Graham Claytor, asked after Marks's mission. Upon discovering that Claytor had received no dispatch about the men in the ocean, Marks gave him the news.

As luck would have it, Claytor, about two hundred miles from the *Indy*'s crew, decided to turn his ship around. He began steaming toward the rescue site at twenty-two and a half knots.

Claytor did this without first radioing his command at Peleliu or asking for orders, a strict violation of his duties as a captain. He was, however, a confident man, with a distinguished record. A lawyer in civilian life, he had been president of the Harvard Law Review and clerk to Supreme Court justice Louis Brandeis before entering the navy in 1942. He was a man used to thinking for himself. At 2:35 p.m., he made contact with Atteberry. He informed him that he expected to arrive sometime after midnight.

Meanwhile, CINCPAC began radioing all ships: BREAK RADIO SILENCE X REPORT YOUR POSITION. The purpose of this dispatch was to determine which ships were in the Philippine Sea. As the responses began flooding into HQ, the *Indy*'s was noticeably absent.

~

Lieutenant Adrian Marks reached the scene of the survivors at 3:20 p.m., and what he found astounded him. Lieutenant Atteberry informed Marks that there were a great many people scattered over a wide area. He said not to drop any lifesaving equipment until he had made a full tour, which Marks quickly did. Both pilots then decided to steer away from the people clinging to rafts and to concentrate on those held up solely by vests. Thirty minutes after he arrived, Marks began showering the men with his provisions.

At about the same time, the destroyers *Ralph Talbot* and *Madison* received orders to cut short their patrols near the island of Ulithi and head directly to the rescue site. Their ETA: twelve hours from the present; sometime early Friday morning.

Marks knew the situation was dire. From his recon altitude of a mere twenty-five feet, he had a clear view to the deep green sea and the hundreds of sharks circling the men. Night, which he knew was the sharks' normal feeding period, was approaching. One of Marks's crewmen watched as a shark attacked one of the men and dragged him under. As Marks himself witnessed more attacks, his anxiety grew. It looked to him as if the survivors were so weak they couldn't even begin to fight back.

Speed was clearly of the essence. Marks skipped the usual communication protocol, sending an uncoded message back to Peleliu. It read: BETWEEN 100 AND 200 SURVIVORS AT POSITION REPORTED. NEED ALL SURVIVAL EQUIPMENT AVAILABLE WHILE DAYLIGHT HOLDS. SURVIVORS MANY WITHOUT RAFTS . . .

In the same message, Marks announced a bold decision: WILL ATTEMPT OPEN SEA LANDING. He had never tried to land in the open sea before. All previous attempts by members of his squadron had ended in disaster. In fact, his squadron was now under standing orders that prohibited making them.

A few minutes later, he yelled into his crew's headsets, checking to make sure they agreed with his decision to attempt a landing. They gave him the thumbs-up. The team was going in.

17

THE FIRST RESCUE

Thursday late afternoon and evening, August 2

Adrian Marks cut the throttle on the seaplane, dramatically lifting the nose of the lumbering amphibious Catalina and setting her down in a power stall. Hitting the top of one wave, the *Playmate 2* was knocked back skyward fifteen feet. Then it came down even harder. At any moment, the plane could blow apart.

On the third touchdown on the ocean she settled down like a hen over an egg, her seams and rivets popping and seawater streaming in. Marks's crew shoved cotton and pencils into the holes in the metal skin of the plane. The radio compartment was taking on water.

The radioman began bailing immediately. The crew joined in, filling ten to twelve buckets an hour. The propellers were still spinning, and it was essential that they didn't dig into the sea, or they would flip the plane.

Marks's copilot, Ensign Irving Lefkovitz, moved to the side hatch and began preparing for rescue. Marks himself had no idea where to steer the plane. The whole craft pitched up and down as if on a carnival ride surrounded by rising and falling walls of water. Circling above, Atteberry became Marks's eyes in the fading twilight. The race was on to collect as many of the survivors as possible before total darkness consumed them all.

Marks had landed among the group led by Dr. Haynes. Their numbers had dwindled from the previous day's 110 to about 95, the group having lost at least 5 more sailors this afternoon. All of them were yelling at the plane, beckoning the pilot to come closer.

Marks gunned the twin engines and powered the PBY through the seas, searching out those near death. It was tricky. The normal taxiing speed of the *Playmate 2* was thirty-five miles per hour, too fast to pick up any men. Marks hit upon a solution. As he gunned the motors, another crew member raised and lowered the landing gear, using them as brakes. It worked.

~

Earlier in the day, upon learning of Gwinn's position coordinates, Captain Granum, back in Leyte, had kicked the rescue effort into high gear. He had confirmed the *Indy*'s departure from Guam. Next he concluded that the latitude and longitude reading corresponded to points she had probably passed over on her trip to Leyte. That she was almost certainly the missing ship in question was becoming clearer by the minute.

Granum issued urgent orders dispatching several patrol vessels and planes to the rescue area. He was now coordinating the rescue operation with the efforts of the Peleliu search and reconnaissance command, from which Gwinn, Atteberry, and Marks had flown.

At the same time the commander of the nearby western Carolines ordered all ships and planes in the vicinity to come to the rescuers' aid.

Shortly before Marks landed in the late afternoon, two B-17 Flying Fortresses from the rescue squadron in Peleliu had arrived at the rescue site. The crew aboard these long-range bombers immediately went to work. They unloaded seventeen life rafts, two twenty-six-foot wooden lifeboats, numerous life vests, and three dozen five-man rubber life rafts to clusters of men in Haynes's group.

Around 7:15 p.m. another PBY also landed. This plane was piloted by Lieutenant Richard Alcorn of the U.S. Army Air Forces. He set down two miles north of Marks and immediately began cruising through the surf, passing dead bodies.

To aid his search in the dusk, Alcorn turned on his plane's light. Mistaking it for survival flares, other planes arriving on the scene began dropping supplies on him. Despite the mishap,

Alcorn was actually able to pick up one survivor before he judged that he could do no good in the dark. He had landed too far afield from most of the survivors anyway.

Alcorn quickly realized, however, that he could be of use by operating his plane's lights as beacons to guide circling aircraft and rescue ships to the scene. He would spend a total of more than fifty-one hours in the area, returning to Peleliu only to refuel.

~

HAYNES'S GROUP

Dr. Haynes, exasperated that his men were still dying with rescue so imminent, knew he had to do something. After Marks had dropped his rafts, Haynes paddled over to one of them. He was too weak to pull the toggle that would self-inflate the craft. In the end, it had taken three sailors to release the cord. They elected Haynes to be the first to board the safe, dry refuge. It was an honor he at first refused, but they were insistent.

After agreeing, Haynes had to remove his bulky life vest, a torturous process. Free from the thing for the first time in nearly four days, his shoulders rubbed raw and bleeding, he clung to the side of the raft. Then he was pushed up by the men in the water and the doctor flopped over the rail. Immediately, he started looking for water on board—he had to find water. But he found none.

He managed to help lift ten more sailors into the raft. A

remaining twenty had to hang on to the lifelines around it. Soon, however, the burning afternoon sun grew unbearable. The men in the raft jumped back into the cooler sea. Their core body temperatures were now dipping below 85 degrees, at which point most major motor functions stumble and cease. That they were functioning at all was a miracle. Haynes thought they all looked like cadavers. The condition of the men was so acute, he knew that they couldn't wait much longer for water.

Haynes's suffering now seemed natural to him. He felt close to God. The doctor felt as if he were about to be lifted up, pinched between two massive, invisible fingers reaching down from the sky. With great mental strain, he tried to operate a desalinating pump stored in the raft but found he had trouble even reading the directions. Yet he didn't give up.

For several long hours he pumped what he thought was potable water, only to discover that each batch was poisoned with the tang of the sea. He cursed his increasing stupidity. In a fit of despair that had been steadily building, he pitched the pump overboard. For the first time since the sinking, he fell to pieces.

The doctor started weeping. He wept angrily over his failure to find water for his sailors, over his inability to keep so many from dying. He felt ashamed that he couldn't do more for them, but he knew he was doing the best he could. And that was all he could ask of himself anymore.

Circling overhead, Lieutenant Commander Atteberry began directing Marks toward micro groups of hard-struggling survivors. The two planes were in constant radio contact as Marks taxied the plane through the swells. Often all he could see were walls of water and then a glimpse of the next wave.

The *Playmate 2*'s side hatch was open, and a Jacob's ladder (a series of steps strung on rope) hung from its lip. A crewman stood on the rungs as Marks handled the plane.

"Okay, Dumbo, come right," radioed Atteberry. "Steady as you go . . . left, a little bit."

"Okay, we see him!" Marks radioed back.

Fearing he might run over a survivor, Marks cut the engines. The crewman on the ladder reached down and grabbed hold of a boy who was floating facedown, gripping his arms and yanking. What he pulled from the sea nauseated him: It was only the upper half of a body. They repeated the taxing process. Often, when the crewmen grabbed hold of the swimmer, they found the boy was too weak to hang on.

Adrian Marks was asking who these men were. He pulled aboard one boy, a petty officer, who told him they were from the *Indianapolis*.

Marks now had the information that for the past five hours had eluded the command back in Peleliu and Guam. But he was too busy to code a message communicating the ship's identity to the outside world. He aimed the plane toward the next cluster of men. The world could wait for the news; he had work to do.

~

As Marks's plane floated past, picking up survivors, Haynes decided to make a try for it. Dr. Haynes didn't really swim as much as claw his way over the water about sixty feet. By the time he reached the rope ladder hanging from Marks's hatch, he was nearly dead.

But he didn't get on the plane. Looking up through blurry eyes, he called out for a beaker of water and a life vest. He pulled the vest on, loosely tying it. Then, pushing the beaker ahead of him as he paddled, he finally made it back to the raft. After downing a small cup, he poured out an allotment and then pointed to a boy. "This is for him," he croaked, his throat parched, before handing the glass down the line of waiting hands.

When the glass came back, Haynes refilled it. And repeated the process, choosing a new boy to drink.

The sight of the water trembling in the glass was excruciating for Haynes; it was all he could do to prevent himself from gulping it all down himself. And by the looks of the sunken, vacant eyes of the rest of the men, he knew that they were all exercising incredible restraint.

As he continued serving them, he felt a blooming sense of pride—not one of these sailors was cheating by drinking out of turn. Haynes would forever marvel over this moment.

Lifting the sailors aboard the *Playmate 2*, Marks discovered that many had swollen, broken legs and arms; boarding was a hideously painful process. At times, as Marks and his crew gave a heave-ho, the flesh of the latest retrieval remained in their hands. The seawater had eaten away all the body hair from some, who came aboard whimpering, pale, and smooth-skinned as newts. Marks and his crew were horrified.

Soon Marks had picked up some thirty men and watched as they were carefully arranged on the deck of the PBY. They thrashed uncontrollably in their delirium, kicking holes in the fuselage. Within a matter of a few hours, the entire water supply would be exhausted.

Each boy was forced to wait several minutes before refilling his cup in order not to upset his shrunken stomach. After two drinks, which totaled just one cup of water, the sailors fell into a deep sleep, broken only by requests for more fluid.

Ed Brown and Bob Gause were hauled aboard, sandwiched between several dozen other men. Brown had spent the day floating and staring at the oblivion of the sky, hallucinating. He was hypnotized by what he saw there. It was a Western Union telegram that stretched from horizon to horizon. It read: DEAR MRS. BROWN, WE REGRET TO INFORM YOU THAT YOUR SON IS MISSING IN ACTION. Now he lay on the plane's deck, overjoyed, even as his rescuers stepped and walked over him.

In his exhaustion, Bob Gause was sitting in several inches of water, remarking that it must really be raining like hell for the inside of the plane to be this wet.

"What do you mean, rain?" said a boy sitting next to him. "It's not raining."

Then the two realized the plane was taking on water; it appeared to be sinking. (The water, in fact, was entering the plane at the seams split during Marks's rough landing.) A number of the sailors started bailing like crazy, fearful they were going to start their ordeal all over again.

Some of the hallucinating sailors had reacted violently to the idea of rescue. Soon the PBY's deck was stacked tight with men kicking senselessly at phantoms. The odor of vomit and excrement filled the plane.

Having run out of room inside the plane, Marks stacked more sailors on the wings. There, they were wrapped mummy-style in parachutes and bound with rope to prevent them from rolling off. By nightfall, he had rescued fifty-six survivors. Approximately three hundred still waited, but darkness, total now, made further rescue efforts impossible. Marks could do no more until daylight; he resolved to wait until the rescue ships arrived.

In usual circumstances Mark's plane could take off again from the water, but now it was too heavy with wounded men to take flight. The pilot would have to wait until a rescue ship arrived to transfer the sailors from his plane onto the ship.

His job was done. The *Playmate 2* drifted through the dark, echoing with the howls of the men stored inside.

18

SHIPS ARRIVE

Early morning to midafternoon, Friday, August 3

Captain Graham Claytor and the *Cecil J. Doyle* steamed into the field of debris and bodies at 11:45 p.m., August 2. Claytor wasted little time getting involved. Lowering a motorized whaleboat, he began off-loading survivors from Marks's PBY into the *Doyle*'s sick bay.

At 12:52 a.m., Friday, August 3, the high-speed transport *Bassett* arrived, and within four hours the destroyers *Ralph Talbot* and *Madison* and the destroyer escort *Dufilho* were also in the area. Although more than twelve hours had passed since Gwinn sighted the survivors, not one of the rescue vessels, except for Marks's, had yet learned the name of the sailors' ship.

During the predawn hours, the *Bassett* would pick up 152 survivors, the single largest group to be plucked from the sea, before being ordered to return to Leyte. These sailors were primarily from the Twible group of rafters, who were drifting about fifteen miles to the northeast of Haynes's swimmers. Between these two floated Captain McVay and his group of nine. Alone, and leading the drift about seven miles to the northwest of Haynes, were McCoy and his four raft mates.

Many, to the amazement of the *Bassett* crewmen, didn't want to be rescued. When the *Bassett* lowered its Higgins boats, the men swimming in the searchlights became convinced that their rescuers were Japanese sailors. (Higgins boats are high-sided, flat-bottomed craft often used by marines for beach landings.) Likewise, the rescue crews, who still didn't know the identity of their catch, weren't so sure a trick wasn't being played on them. All they could see were oil-blackened faces and the whites of deeply sunken eyes staring back at them. Drawing his pistol, one rescuer yelled out, "Hey! What city do the Dodgers play in?"

"Brooklyn!" came the reply. The crew gunned its boat ahead to the rescue.

To get the sailors aboard required some imaginative thinking. One rescuer convinced the survivors he was taking them to a dance and made them form a conga line leading to the Higgins boat. Others were told they were heading out for a night of liberty on the town.

Twenty-year-old *Bassett* rescuer William Van Wilpe was

uncommonly brave, jumping into the sea from his boat after three survivors had fallen out. They sank immediately, dead weight. Van Wilpe emerged on the surface carrying all three in his arms, a Herculean effort. Later, when he dislocated his shoulder, he popped it back into place himself and quickly resumed his duty.

One survivor, Jack Miner, tried feverishly to swim away from the approach of a Higgins boat, but was too weak. He was pulled over the rail of the craft, kicking and struggling. Lifted up by a burly, bearded sailor, Miner believed he was in the arms of the angel Gabriel. He stopped struggling when a slice of orange was shoved in his mouth. To Miner the fruit tasted like heaven, and when he finished it, he sucked greedily on the rind.

~

At 4:00 a.m., the searchlight of the *Cecil J. Doyle* found Dr. Haynes's raft in its sharp beam.

Sitting next to the doctor was one of his men who was mentally incapacitated. "Hey," the kid yelled up to the *Doyle*. "Have you got any water on board?"

The eager answer came back, "We got a lot of water on board!"

The kid was silent. After a moment, he said, "'Cause if you ain't got any water, go away and leave us alone!"

A cargo net was rolled down the metal hull of the *Doyle*.

Haynes was hauled from the sea with a rope tied around his waist. He was naked, burned, and delirious. But he pushed away the men holding him up, announcing: "I can stand on my own!"

"Who are you?" Claytor asked him.

"This is all that's left of the *Indianapolis*," Dr. Haynes rasped. "We have been in the water four days."

Captain Claytor was astounded by the news that he was rescuing the men of the USS *Indianapolis*. As fate would have it, he now realized, he had actually been searching for one of his own relatives: Captain McVay was married to Claytor's cousin.

The previous evening, before arriving on the scene, Claytor had received a bulletin from the Philippine Sea Frontier: 1ST VESSEL ON SCENE ADVISE IDENTITY OF SHIP SURVIVORS AND CAUSE OF SINKING. Now, in the early hours of Friday, August 3, Claytor was finally able to spread the word.

At 12:30 a.m., Claytor radioed the commander of the western Carolines: HAVE ARRIVED AREA X AM PICKING UP SURVIVORS FROM THE USS INDIANAPOLIS, TORPEODOED [*sic*] AND SUNK LAST SUNDAY NIGHT.

The news was a stunning blow. It quickly rippled all the way back to Pearl Harbor and to Admiral Ernest King, chief of naval operations, in Washington, D.C. Both King and Admiral Nimitz, in particular, were concerned about the impact of the tragedy on the impending plans to bomb Japan. They feared a controversy in the midst of what could be the war's—and the navy's—finest hour.

On the same day that the remainder of the *Indy*'s men were being rescued, President Truman was bound from London to the States aboard the cruiser *Augusta*. He was returning from the Potsdam Conference. That was the meeting that united Great Britain, Russia, and the United States in the final fight against Japan.

On board the ship, gathering a few reporters around him, Truman announced that America had a new kind of weapon that could end the war.

By this time, the last components of Little Boy had arrived on Tinian for final assembly. Hiroshima would be its target. But off Guam and Tinian, the weather was worsening. Heavy seas limited B-29 strikes on Japan and complicated scheduling an actual bombing date. The crew of the *Enola Gay*—the B-29 that was to drop the bomb—was forced to wait for clear skies.

~

Back in the waters of the South Pacific, the search continued at full speed. With the aid of powerful spotlights, as many as seven rescue planes circled over the site in coordinated patterns. They directed the ships' efforts below. Using Higgins boats, motor launches, and Stokes stretchers (wire baskets) lowered by the ships' cranes, the sailors were retrieved, one by painful one.

The crew of the *Bassett* was awestruck by what it found. Some of the men pulled aboard were so hideously disfigured that their rescuers, most of whom were about the same age as the survivors, broke down and wept as they hauled the living corpses aboard.

At 4:30 a.m. on August 3, the destroyer USS *Madison* became command central, taking over from the debilitated *Playmate 2*. At 6:30 a.m., the survivors were off-loaded from the *Playmate 2*. Then the plane's crew removed the salvage gear from their craft, took one last look around, and boarded a motor launch, which took them to a waiting rescue ship, the *Cecil J. Doyle*.

They were leaving the plane behind. The PBY was covered with scars and slits in her metal skin from the pounding of the waves she'd endured on landing. The massive plane was leaking oil out her belly, and her wings were dented and punctured; she would never fly again.

To keep the plane from falling into the hands of the Japanese, she had to be destroyed. On board the *Doyle*, Marks watched as the ship's antiaircraft guns—the deck-mounted 40 mms— opened up and riddled the plane. Then he bade the *Playmate 2* goodbye as she sank.

~

The rescue ships were a mess. A slippery film of seawater and fuel oil coated the decks, and dead bodies were laid in rows on the sterns. The survivors were fed fruit and water. They were treated for exhaustion, dehydration, shark bites, saltwater ulcers, shock, burns, and malnutrition. (A healthy nineteen-year-old boy usually carries about 20 percent body fat; many of the survivors had lost an estimated 14 percent of theirs. Over the course of the four days, one sailor had lost more than thirty-five pounds.)

The survivors were led to showers where they were doused with diesel fuel to remove the oil that clung stubbornly to their bodies. Many of the sailors only began to realize they had been rescued when the diesel fuel was rinsed off with freshwater. They laughed with joy, then fell into fits of weeping.

The crew of the *Doyle* moved out of its bunks. They gave the survivors fresh underwear and T-shirts and waited on them hand and foot throughout the night. Coffee, soup, ice cream, and fruit were all made available.

In the wardroom, Adrian Marks found himself alone with Haynes. The doctor chattered fast and furiously in a hoarse whisper about the past days' events. He seemed compelled to get his story out as quickly as possible.

"Doctor," Marks asked, trying to offer comfort, "why don't you rest? Your voice is almost gone. You can tell it tomorrow."

But Haynes, who couldn't stop crying, continued talking, questions flooding out of him. "Why didn't they know we were missing?" he kept asking. "Why weren't they looking for us? Why! Why! Why!"

After being led to the shower, Haynes finally fell silent. He sat back on a stool and opened his mouth before the water hit. Desperately, he tried to lick the freshwater right out of the air. In spite of the excruciating pain of the scrubbing, he started to giggle hysterically, like a child.

~

By midafternoon on August 3, the aftershocks of the disaster were rippling through the naval command. The following order was relayed to all ships: UNTIL FURTHER ORDERS ALL SHIPS WITH 500 OR MORE TOTAL PERSONNEL ON BOARD SHALL BE PROVIDED WITH AN ESCORT BETWEEN ULITHI AND LEYTE REGARDLESS OF SPEED.

The Philippine Sea Frontier at Leyte, to which the *Indy* had been headed, also issued this directive: ALL COMBATANT SHIPS 5 HOURS OVERDUE SAHLL [*sic*] BE REPORTED TO ORIGINATOR.

Fine rules, but too late for the sailors of the *Indianapolis*.

FROM ONE KIND OF
FEAR TO ANOTHER

Early morning to midafternoon, Friday, August 3

McVAY'S GROUP

By the early morning of August 3, Captain McVay still had not been found.

It had been a sleepless night for the captain and his crew. John Spinelli was lying listlessly in the raft, dreaming of eating candied Bing cherries. "Dear Lord," he prayed, "thank you for getting me this far."

McVay wondered just how much longer they could hold on. At about midnight the night before, his spirits had lifted when he spotted the faint searchlight of the *Doyle* ten miles away. He finally understood without a doubt that a search-and-rescue effort was underway. The earlier planes had not been a fluke—they were actually looking for him and his men. Others had likely made it off the *Indy*; he was overjoyed.

But who could say if his group would be found? With so much ocean, it would be hard, he knew. They were constantly drifting to the south and east. Since about 12:30 a.m., Monday, July 30, McVay and his flotilla had drifted a total of about 116 miles.

This morning there were planes executing what looked like a box pattern. They were cruising in regular opposing lines overhead, scrutinizing every mile beneath them.

McVay fired a flare—he was down to a precious remaining few. But none of the planes noticed. He and the men looked on as the search continued in the distance. They were frantic.

Suddenly one of the men croaked, "Fellows?" Nobody turned—all eyes were on the planes. "Fellows," he repeated. "Do I see a ship, or am I hallucinating?"

McVay looked up in surprise. There was a ship bearing down on them, its bow throwing a crisp white wake. McVay stood and started waving wildly, shouting, "Here! Over here!"

It was close to 10:00 a.m. The ship was the high-speed transport *Ringness*. It had picked up a blip—a light indicating an object—on its radar screen at over 4,000 yards (about 2.25 miles) and steadily tracked it. It was a stroke of unimaginable luck for McVay and the men. The blip had been triggered by an ammunition can that the captain had used earlier to make a failed smudge pot that he hoped would emit smoke. Into the can, he had shredded a cotton-like substance called kapok torn from a life vest. He ignited the fiber with a shot from his flare gun. Although not in the way he intended, the smudge pot had saved them.

The *Ringness* arrived at McVay's raft. After more than four days afloat, with no more than slivers of Spam and some malted milk tablets to eat, McVay's group was saved. The captain managed to climb up the Jacob's ladder over the side of the *Ringness* under his own power.

Once on deck, he and the exhausted crew were whisked to the ship's sick bay. A pharmacist's mate checked their blood pressure and heart rates. All of McVay's group had fared remarkably well.

The sailors were showered and given fresh jeans. A clean uniform was found for McVay. John Spinelli was amazed that even the *Ringness*'s officers were helping scrub down the dirty survivors. He had never been more grateful. But he found the news of the scope of the disaster unsettling. As Spinelli tried to get some rest in a bunk, each crashing wave against the ship's hull brought back vivid, unwelcome flashbacks to the torpedoing.

McVay was placed in a private cabin. When the *Ringness* commander, Captain Meyer entered, he found McVay lying on the bed.

Meyer sat in a chair. After a moment, McVay volunteered that he wanted to talk about what had happened. Meyer had prepared a dispatch describing the *Indy*'s torpedoing to be radioed to CINCPAC at Pearl Harbor, and he read it aloud. It included the words *not zigzagging*—the evasive method of movement to make it more difficult for a torpedo to find its mark.

McVay requested the words be omitted. Meyer was understanding yet persuasive in his argument to let the words stand. Seeing that McVay was traumatized, Meyer reminded him that the truth of what had happened would come to light at a court of inquiry, which the two captains knew was imminent.

McVay agreed. It was the right thing to do.

After Meyer left the cabin, McVay was alone with his thoughts. And fears: the prospect of life after the disaster. What a captain dreads most had happened. With his ship gone, he could sense that his career might soon disappear as well.

~

Shortly thereafter, the two destroyers, *Madison* and *Ralph Talbot*, along with the destroyer escort *Dufilho*, formed a 3.5-mile-long scouting line. They combed the area, searching through the night.

The transport ships *Register* and *Ringness* steamed for Peleliu and the makeshift hospital there (the *Doyle* had departed for the island earlier). By the end of the day, Admiral Nimitz would order the hospital ship *Tranquillity*, presently anchored off Ulithi, to Peleliu. It would be used for transporting the survivors to the more substantial Base 18 Hospital on Guam.

The search, which had been in progress for over twenty-four hours, was nearing a close.

~

McCOY'S GROUP

McCoy was certain that he had died long ago, maybe yesterday, maybe the previous night. It was hard to tell. His throat was on fire; he regretted every ounce of water he'd ever wasted. He, Brundige, Payne, Outland, and Gray drifted in their raft, barely alive.

The entire previous day, they'd watched the planes circle, knowing that a rescue effort was underway. After the sun had gone down, they had spotted what they thought was a ship's wobbly searchlight. All night long, they had stared at the light in silence. It rose straight from the sea, pencil-thin, and flattened against the ceiling of clouds.

But McCoy and Brundige didn't let the light out of their sight; they could practically reach out and touch it. They hoped and prayed it meant rescue, but rescue never came.

Now, on the morning of August 3, Brundige spotted more planes on the horizon. "Look, they came back, just like you'd said," he told McCoy. "But they're not coming our way."

"They will," said McCoy. "They will. They gotta work their way around to us."

As the day wore on, the planes got smaller and smaller in the sky. And then they disappeared. Gone. No one was coming. No one.

Imagine feeling everyone else was rescued, but you were

forgotten, left to die. McCoy and Brundige started to weep. They pressed close to the tied-together mass that was Payne, Outland, and Gray, and added their vests' straps to the cluster. Now all five were floating inside the raft as one, foreheads touching.

"We're gonna go out of our gourds," said McCoy. "We're gonna die. But at least this way we won't fall over and drown in our vests." It was taking longer to die than McCoy expected.

And then, near dusk, he heard a noise. It was a plane. *Not another one,* he thought. *Not another goddamned plane that won't see us.*

But not only had it seen them, it was coming right at them. Fifty feet off the water, a Catalina seaplane passed over so close that McCoy could even see the guy inside its clear bubble blister. He was yelling something and pointing down at them. The plane banked sharply and circled. Then, on its second pass, a dye bomb was tossed out the hatch. It sent a chartreuse plume spreading around their raft.

And then the plane flew away. McCoy knew they had been spotted, but were they actually going to be picked up? He trusted nothing, and no one. Still, he felt lighter, alive. He knew he was coming back from the dead, and it was a wonderful feeling.

Out of nowhere a ship appeared. One moment, the sea was empty, twilight crawling across it; the next, there stood the massive gray hull of what looked like a transport ship. A guy on deck spun a line overhead and tossed it far out. On the end of it was a monkey fist, a lead weight wrapped with twine.

It was an excellent shot; the fist landed directly at McCoy's side. He grabbed it and squeezed, crying out, "You found us! I can't believe you found us!"

After an unsuccessful attempt to reel in the raft, two of the ship's crew members jumped into the water and started swimming. They didn't get far, though; once they spotted the sharks circling the raft, they turned around and scrambled up the net on the ship's side. McCoy couldn't believe it. These guys were going to let a few sharks scare them off? He'd seen *sharks*.

He watched in grateful amazement as two more jumped overboard without hesitation and stroked up to them, knives in their hands. As they began cutting at the vests' straps and separating the five sailors, McCoy, dazed, kept repeating, "I just can't believe you found us! You found us! *You found us!*"

His crew of four were covered in oil and burned, their faces swollen beyond recognition. McCoy himself was severely dehydrated. The outlines of his ribs and cheekbones were visible through his skin. His tongue, sunburned, protruded from his mouth. He shaded it like a man cupping a flame from the wind.

The two crewmen towed them to the waiting rescue ship, the *Ringness*, where a boatswain's chair (resembling a child's swing) was lowered down by crane. They were lifted aboard. All except McCoy. He insisted on climbing up the net ladder. When the marine reached the top, he was so weak he fell to the deck; kissing it, he burst into tears. He tried rising again but found he couldn't. He was unable to stop crying.

McCoy was carried by stretcher to a shower, where the

Ringness crew began the long, painful bath. He was then led to a bunk in the crew's quarters and fed water from a spoon for an hour. Never in his life had anything tasted so sweet. He lay there savoring the small sips. Finally he fell asleep. He tumbled into a deep and soundless chasm of peace, where he lay for twenty hours.

McCoy and his raft mates were the last crew members of the USS *Indianapolis* to be rescued. They had spent about 112 hours—or more than four and a half days—adrift without food, water, or shelter from the sun. His group of five had drifted the farthest of any of the survivors, an astounding 124 miles. As they slept in their bunks aboard the USS *Ringness*, they resembled sunburned skeletons more than the young men they were.

RECOVERY

Saturday, August 4, to Wednesday, August 15, 1945

By the following day, Saturday, August 4, the armada of rescue boats and planes had combed hundreds of square miles of ocean.

During the afternoon, rescue crews received a scare. The *Dufilho* reported solid underwater sonar contact with a Japanese submarine. The destroyer performed a depth charge attack, but it was without result. The rescue effort resumed. No other survivors were discovered, however, and by 5:00 p.m. the search seemed to be concluded.

In all, the *Cecil J. Doyle* collected 93 men, including the 56 men Marks had hauled aboard the *Playmate 2*. The high-speed transports USS *Register* and USS *Ringness* picked up a total of 51 survivors. Among them was Mike Kuryla, who'd been in one of the three rafts cut free from McCoy's and set adrift.

The USS *Bassett* posted a whopping 152 saved, including the Twible rafters group. The destroyer escort USS *Dufilho* and the destroyer USS *Ralph Talbot* picked up 25 survivors between them.

The casualties were astounding, and the death toll rattled the battled-hardened crews of the rescue ships. Of the 1,196 passengers who had sailed from Guam, only 320 had survived the torpedoing and long ordeal at sea.

In less than a week, four more would die in military hospitals, reducing the total number of survivors to 316. Of the nearly 900 men who died, it's probable that 200 were victims of shark attacks, an average of 50 men a day. In all, 880 men were lost.

Pilot Adrian Marks would be haunted by the sight of the sharks and the conditions of the rescue for the rest of his days. "I will never forget how dark were the early hours of that night," he later remarked. "There was no moon and the starlight was obscured by clouds. And even though we were near the equator, the wind whipped up and it was cold. We had long since dispensed the last drop of water. Scores of badly injured men, stacked three deep in the fuselage and ranged far out on both wings [of his aircraft], were softly crying with thirst and with pain."

As for McCoy, he would always wonder about those sailors who might've been left behind. "They were basically all done looking when they found us," he would say. "I wonder how many were left out there and just watched those ships and planes finally disappear from sight. We couldn't have lasted another day."

~

On Saturday, August 4, reconnaissance ships started the work of retrieving and identifying dead bodies.

The logbooks of the four principal ships involved—the destroyer escorts *French* and *Alvin C. Cockrell*, and the destroyers *Helm* and *Aylwin*—read like something from a horror movie. The *Helm* carried the following report for its August 4–5 patrol:

"All bodies were in extremely bad condition and had been dead for an estimated 4 or 5 days. Some had life jackets and life belts, most had nothing. About half of the bodies were shark-bitten, some to such a degree that they more nearly resembled skeletons. From one to four sharks were attacking a body not more than fifty yards from the ship, and continued to do so until driven off by rifle fire.

For the most part it was impossible to get finger prints from the bodies as the skin had come off the hands or the hands were lacerated by sharks. Skin was removed from the hands of bodies containing no identification, when possible, and the Medical Officer will dehydrate the skin and attempt to make legible prints.

All personal effects [were] removed from the bodies for purposes of identification. After examination, all bodies were sunk, using two-inch line and a weight of three 5-inch/38-caliber projectiles. There were still more bodies in the area when darkness brought a close to the gruesome operations for the day. In all, twenty-eight bodies were examined and sunk."

A total of about ninety-one bodies would be retrieved by the ships and buried at sea, with identification made whenever possible. Not until August 9, after searching hundreds of miles of ocean, would the last ship leave the area.

~

As the USS *Ringness* had made its way through the night of August 3 across the Philippine Sea, Captain McVay watched the lights on Peleliu draw near. He must have sensed that he was turning to a new fight for survival, this time with the navy. Minutes before the ship docked, he had stood on the bridge and with a shaking voice told his rescuers, on behalf of all the *Indianapolis* crew, how grateful he was.

Captain Meyer thought he had never seen such humility and compassion in an officer.

On Peleliu, a news blackout was ordered: No information about the sinking would leak from the island. Marine guards blocked access to the wooden hospital barracks where the men were convalescing. No word would leak to the outside world that 1,196 U.S. sailors had been lost and forgotten at sea for nearly five days.

On Sunday, August 5, McVay held a press conference. But

everything he said—as well as any news stories written by correspondents on the island—was subject to the scrutiny of military censors. Not a word of McVay's press conference would be released until after the war. Regular wartime news protocols still very much applied.

At the news conference a reporter asked the captain, "What would be the normal time before you would be reported overdue?"

"That is a question I would like to ask someone," McVay shot back. "A ship that size practically runs on a train schedule. I should think by noon [on Tuesday], they would have started to call by radio to find out where we were, or if something was wrong. This is something I want to ask somebody myself—why didn't this get out sooner?"

This was as close to a public condemnation of the navy as the captain would ever allow himself to make.

~

The following day, Monday, August 6, 1945, the *Enola Gay* took off from the airstrip at Tinian Island. At 8:15 a.m. the plane dropped Little Boy on Hiroshima. A member of its assembly team had written on its side: "This one is for the Boys of the *Indianapolis*."

More than 118,000 Japanese of the city's estimated population of 350,000 were killed by the world's first atomic bomb. (A total of 140,000 would be dead as a result of its aftereffects by the end of the year.) Temperatures at the epicenter of the explosion exceeded 1 million degrees, and winds of up to 500 miles per hour were whipped up by the blast.

~

By Wednesday, August 8, McVay, Haynes, McCoy, and all the other survivors had been reunited at the Base 18 Hospital in Guam. Still under marine guard, they were not allowed to talk with any unauthorized personnel about their ordeal. McVay, who didn't need direct medical attention and was billeted at officers' quarters, visited with the men in the enlisted men's hospital barracks. They were overjoyed to see him, profoundly glad that he had survived the ordeal. Their captain, looking fit and rested, betrayed no emotion about the trouble brewing.

Many of the sailors recovered at a rapid rate and soon were playing basketball and baseball on the base. Others were not so lucky. The saltwater ulcers covering their broken arms and legs had eaten the muscle to the bone. One boy's ears had been fried to the texture of cornflakes by the sun.

Dr. Haynes would require a month of convalescence before walking again. His feet, burned by the flash fires of the torpedoing, were painfully tender, as were the third-degree burns on his hands and face.

Private McCoy was nourished by a diet of ice water and raw eggs. His head was shaved to remove his oil-matted hair. He also was undergoing a daily, painful treatment on his face. It involved a nurse cracking open the burned, dried skin and peeling it away with tweezers to apply an antiseptic ointment. Fortunately, the nurse would peel off just one side of his face each day.

Admiral Spruance, commander of the navy's Fifth Fleet, paid a visit to the hospital. The sailors lined up and he pinned Purple Hearts on their hospital pajamas. They were profoundly moved as he went from bed to bed shaking hands, offering congratulations. The admiral even stopped to play a few hands of hearts with some of the sailors.

On Guam, the purpose of the *Indy*'s record-breaking voyage across the Pacific to Tinian was finally revealed to the officers of the ship. Dr. Haynes was lying in his hospital bed when an army medical officer approached and asked if he could have a word.

"I know who you are!" said Haynes, recognizing the man. He was James Nolan. Haynes had last seen him posing as an artillery officer aboard the *Indy* during the trip from San Francisco to Tinian. Nolan explained that he was actually an army medical officer specializing in radiation medicine. Then he informed Haynes that the *Indy* had carried the bomb dropped on Hiroshima. Haynes said little; in fact, he found he had no reaction at all. Like many of the crew, he simply would be glad when the war was over.

On Thursday, August 9, a second atomic bomb, this one named Fat Man, was dropped on Nagasaki. The blast of the horrible weapon killed 40,000 Japanese and wounded another 60,000. On the following day, August 10, Japan sued for peace.

~

On August 9, Admiral Nimitz, from his office in Guam, called for a court of inquiry concerning the sinking of the *Indianapolis*. Nimitz asked that this proceeding start in less than a week.

The inquiry would investigate the cause of the disaster, the reason for the rescue delay, and determine what culpability, if any, existed among those involved. This was regular procedure in the aftermath of any possible violation of military law.

But amazingly, one of the judges sitting at the inquiry would be Vice Admiral Murray, commander of the Marianas in Guam. When the *Indy* was getting ready to leave Guam, he and his subordinate Oliver Naquin had withheld information. It was under Murray's command that McVay received the incomplete intelligence report concerning enemy submarine activity along the Peddie route.

~

At 8:00 p.m. on August 14, 1945, President Truman stepped into the Rose Garden and triumphantly declared the end of World War II into a bouquet of microphones. After nearly four years of fighting, it was finally over.

Some of the *Indy*'s sailors sat up in bed and cheered at the news as it was announced over the hospital's loudspeakers. It had been twelve days since the first men were rescued. The sinking was still a secret. No one, except U.S. military brass and some hospital workers on the islands of Samar and Peleliu, knew of the disaster. This was about to change.

Minutes before Truman's announcement, the White House released this terse bulletin: "The USS *Indianapolis* has been lost in the Philippine Sea as the result of enemy action. The next of kin of casualties have been notified."

Some families first learned the dreaded news as they were gathered around radios listening to Truman's speech. McCoy's mother was met at her home in St. Louis, Missouri, by a marine bearing word that her son was missing in action. (A number of the survivors' families first received telegrams that their sons were missing, and these mistakes were corrected by follow-up telegrams.) She told the marine, "No, sir, I know my son's all right," and then she slammed the door.

The news of the *Indy* sinking did not entirely surprise Mrs. McCoy. On the night the ship sank, she had sat straight up in bed, convinced that something terrible was happening to her son. "Giles," she said, shaking her husband awake. "Giles Jr. is in trouble, I know it."

In Fairfield, Connecticut, Dr. Haynes's wife received a telegram that read: A REPORT JUST RECEIVED SHOWS YOUR HUSBAND HAS BEEN WOUNDED IN ACTION 30 JULY 1945. DIAGNOSIS: EXHAUSTION FROM OVER-EXPOSURE . . . YOUR ANXIETY IS APPRECIATED.

Mrs. Haynes soon received a second telegram, this one from

her husband. He was unhappily convalescing in a wheelchair on Guam. INJURY IS NOT SERIOUS, Haynes wrote. AM GETTING ALONG ALL RIGHT. ALL MY LOVE, LEW.

On August 15, military censorship of the war's news was lifted, and the newspapers were subsequently filled with stories about the *Indy*. The *New York Times* called the sinking "one of the darkest pages of our naval history." Newspapers across the country soon echoed the sentiment.

The public was saddened and bewildered. How could such a calamity occur so close to the end of the war?

These news stories were soon buried, however, by larger headlines recounting America's victory. On V-J Day (Victory over Japan), celebrations consumed the country. Whether the navy's timing of its announcement of the *Indy*'s sinking was by design or happenstance, the effect was the same: The public quickly forgot the disaster.

The families of the sailors who died in the sinking, however, demanded explanations. The navy, as of yet, had few answers— but it was looking for them.

EPILOGUE

On August 13, 1945, the court of inquiry's proceedings opened at the headquarters of the commander on Guam. McVay rode there with Giles McCoy, who was now his personal driver. The captain had visited the young marine in the hospital. There he offered him the job because he was aware of McCoy's loyal service.

As their jeep climbed up the steep CINCPAC hill, McVay asked McCoy how he'd fared in the water.

"Fine, sir. I got along just fine."

"Well, we were damn lucky to survive." He paused. "You know what? I think they're going to put it to me."

McCoy asked what he was suggesting.

McVay replied that he suspected that the navy was going to pin blame on him for the sinking, using his failure to zigzag as an excuse.

On August 20, after hearing the testimony of forty-three witnesses, the inquiry ended. The court had pored over the minutiae of the case, including the question of the incomplete intelligence reports McVay received at Guam before sailing.

Captain Oliver Naquin, who was one of the people who withheld information from McVay, was a witness. Naquin testified that he had felt the danger of an enemy sub attack was "practically negligible." And the court believed him.

Also under consideration was the failure of the port director at Leyte to report the *Indy*'s non-arrival at her scheduled ETA. It found this circumstance regrettable, but understandable due to the ambiguous nature of the navy directive regarding the non-arrival of combatant ships.

The court primarily blamed the sinking and ensuing deaths of the crew on two things: McVay's failure to zigzag in conditions that it considered "good with intermittent moonlight"; and his failure to send out a distress message.

McVay himself testified that he doubted a message had left the ship during the short time it took to sink. The testimony of Radio Technician Jack Miner, who witnessed the SOS message leaving the transmitter during the sinking, was apparently disregarded.

Also found to be at fault were Rear Admiral McCormick's staff for their incorrect decoding of the message notifying him of the *Indy*'s impending arrival in Leyte. Lieutenant Stewart Gibson was found at fault for failing to report that the *Indy* had not met her ETA. The court recommended disciplinary action for McCormick's staff and a letter of admonition for Gibson.

For McVay, it recommended court-martial.

The matter was now in the hands of the secretary of the navy, James Forrestal, who would decide if legal action should proceed.

~

In early September, after nearly a month of convalescence on Guam, the survivors boarded the carrier escort *Hollandia* and set sail for the United States.

On September 26 they were met in San Diego by a meager homecoming parade sponsored by the local Salvation Army, which handed out miniature bottles of milk to the sailors as they walked off the ship. Most of them had no interest in taking part in the festivities. Generally speaking, they did not share the postwar jubilation that swept up most of the five million soldiers returning home. The sinking and disaster had tainted their experience.

McCoy went home on a two-week leave to his mother, father, and three sisters in Missouri. He tried to put the war as far in his past as possible but remained on active duty, with another two years to serve. He did not relish this prospect.

Dr. Haynes had no intention of quitting. But he did return to Connecticut for a thirty-day leave with his wife. At home, he met his newborn son for the first time.

Captain McVay had flown to Washington, D.C., in early September. He tried hard to convey his sense of grief and loss in letters he wrote to the bereaved families, which he composed in a temporary office in the navy yard while the investigation into the *Indy*'s sinking continued. He was consumed with guilt over the deaths of so many young men. His punishment, he felt, would be a long life.

On November 29, close to four months after his rescue, McVay learned that he was to be court-martialed. The trial would begin in five days, on Monday, December 3, 1945.

Admiral Nimitz and Admiral Spruance had disagreed with the inquiry's initial recommendation and suggested a letter of reprimand. However, the chief of naval operations, Admiral King, a stern and "by the book" navy man, pressed for the trial, and Secretary Forrestal agreed.

Unbelievably, the navy had not yet finalized the charges. In fact, the navy's Judge Advocate General (JAG) sent Forrestal a memo explaining that only one of the inquiry's contemplated charges could be proved. Because McVay had already admitted during the inquiry that he wasn't zigzagging before the torpedoing, a trial was not actually necessary to convict him on this charge. Nevertheless, they called it Charge I.

Consulting with Forrestal, the JAG omitted the inquiry's charge that McVay failed to send a distress signal. In its place they agreed to charge him with "failure to abandon ship in a timely manner." They called this Charge II. Making this charge stick, however, was problematic. Since the ship had gone down so quickly, it could be difficult to prove the difference between a "timely" and "untimely" abandonment.

In reality, they had little choice. Without a second, halfway viable charge, they had no trial; sentencing of McVay on Charge I could have taken place immediately.

"It is, therefore, respectfully submitted," the JAG explained to Forrestal, "that Charge II (failure to abandon ship in a timely manner) should not be omitted, despite the fact the evidence may be held insufficient. Full justification for ordering the trial on Charge II springs from the fact this case is of vital interest not only to the families of those who lost their lives, but also to the public at large."

McVay had less than a week to prepare his defense. King was eager to hurry the proceedings. He had refused the captain his first choice of counsel when his preferred lawyer proved not immediately available. McVay ended up with an inexperienced lawyer.

Before the trial, McVay was asked by a news reporter what he thought the outcome might be. "I was in command of the ship," he replied, "and I am responsible for its fate. I hope they make their decisions soon, and do what they want with me."

As it turned out, then, the question as to why nine hundred U.S. sailors were left to float for as many as five days in a hostile ocean would not be considered by the court. That is, the conduct of the navy would not be on trial.

This legal sleight of hand had been achieved by the navy's careful selection of charges. By law, all questions to the court had to pertain only to the two it had drawn—"failure to order abandon ship in a timely manner" and "hazarding his ship by failing to zigzag." There was no possibility of the establishment of navy culpability.

Still, by and large, the American public sensed that McVay was getting a raw deal. *Time* magazine suggested that the tragedy of the sinking represented a "colossal blunder" by the navy.

On December 3, 1945, Charles Butler McVay's court-martial convened in a converted classroom at the Washington navy yard. Such trials were usually semiprivate affairs executed swiftly out of public view. On the morning of McVay's trial, the courtroom was filled with reporters, photographers, and citizens. They were curious to get a glimpse of the first captain in U.S. history to be court-martialed for losing his ship as the result of an act of war.

The proceedings were well orchestrated and got swiftly underway. McVay sat stiffly in his chair in a spotless uniform, nervously fiddling with a pencil, sensing the walls closing in on his career.

Called to testify, Dr. Haynes found McVay a forlorn version of his former self. On the stand, the JAG lawyer wouldn't allow Haynes to talk about the sailors' time in the water but asked instead about visibility on the night of the sinking. The good doctor told the prosecutor that, yes, visibility on the night of the sinking was poor; in fact, all the survivors called to the witness stand provided testimony to this effect.

In rebuttal, the prosecution argued that conditions were clear enough for the *Indy* to be sunk; therefore, visibility at some point was at least partially clear. The trial was not going well for McVay—the prosecution was driving home Charge I.

What McVay didn't know was that his counsel was missing the one piece of evidence that might have acquitted him. McVay and his lawyer were unaware of the ULTRA intelligence that had been withheld from McVay during his meeting with Captain Oliver Naquin.

A report labeled SECRET and sent to Admiral King by the navy inspector general had blamed the navy for failure to make full use of this intelligence. It had also explained that it would be necessary for the prosecution to return to Guam in order to fully explore the situation. King, in his haste to get the trial underway, chose to disregard the report. From the navy's point of view, the ULTRA intelligence that was gained by cracking the enemy's coded messages wasn't entered into testimony because it was so top secret that, in essence, it didn't exist.

During the trial's second week, it seemed that McVay's fate might change.

The navy made the surreal prosecutorial decision to fly Mochitsura Hashimoto—the commander of the sub that sank the *Indy*—from Japan to Washington to testify against the captain. His presence in the courtroom raised an uproar among politicians and citizens, and in newspapers across the country. *Newsweek* carried an editorial from the *Army and Navy Bulletin* declaring that "responsibility for the debacle . . . must be fixed several echelons higher than a lone commanding officer." On the floor of the House of Representatives, Massachusetts Congressperson Edith Rogers called Hashimoto's presence an "outrage against justice" and demanded his testimony be stricken.

Nevertheless, the prosecution explained that Hashimoto's testimony was crucial. They needed to know "what he saw, what he did, and how he did it" on the night of the sinking. This, they said, was relevant to the charge that the captain endangered his ship by failing to zigzag.

The assembled panel of seven navy admirals agreed, and Hashimoto was allowed to proceed. Dressed in an ill-fitting blue suit, the visibly uncomfortable commander made his way to the witness stand, where he quickly proceeded to embarrass the navy by explaining that zigzagging would have made "no change in [the] method in firing the torpedoes." He would have sunk the *Indianapolis* no matter what course she was on.

A few days later, the prosecution was dealt an apparent second blow by the testimony of the highly decorated American submarine commander Glynn Donaho. Asked to describe the usefulness of zigzagging as a defensive maneuver, the respected commander explained that the move was of negligible value.

Nonetheless, after two weeks of testimony, on December 19, Charles Butler McVay was convicted of "hazarding his ship by failing to zigzag." As the navy JAG had suspected, he was acquitted of the charge of "failing to sound abandon ship in a timely manner."

McVay was demoted one hundred points in permanent rank and another hundred in temporary rank, which meant he would never become an admiral. In view of his outstanding service, however, Admiral King and Admiral Nimitz recommended his sentence be remitted, or, in effect, suspended. (Technically, McVay could have been fined or dismissed from service.)

Four other officers were also punished. Lieutenant Stewart Gibson received a letter of reprimand, while his superior officer, Leyte Port Director Jules Sancho, received a milder letter of admonition. Captain Alfred Granum and his ranking officer, Commodore Norman Gillette, acting commander of the Philippine Sea Frontier, also received letters of reprimand.

McVay had received the announcement of his sentence standing ramrod straight without a hint of emotion. He was a navy man, and he would live and die by its rules; it was as natural to him as breathing. And yet, his naval career was over. He would never command another ship. He left the courtroom on Louise's arm, looking stonily composed.

Back at home, through the Christmas season, the captain began receiving hate mail. Letters to him had comments such as "Merry Christmas! Our family's holiday would be a lot merrier if you hadn't killed my son." McVay would continue to receive letters for the rest of his life. Louise made it a point to patrol the day's mail pile and remove the bitter correspondence. If she didn't, McVay would bundle the letters with rubber bands and tuck them in his dresser drawer, as if forever wanting to remind himself of his guilt.

Three months after the court-martial, he left Washington.

～

In the aftermath of Captain McVay's court-martial, some of the survivors returned to military service, while others drifted back into civilian life. Many got lucky, put the disaster behind them, and joined the postwar American boom. John Spinelli, who'd floated under the captain's watchful eye, moved back to New Mexico with his wife and new daughter. He became a butcher, then worked for thirty-seven years reading utility meters.

Others became nightclub owners, bricklayers, or electricians. Jack Miner took over his father's paper company. Mike Kuryla worked for a construction company in Chicago, and Ed Brown became a traveling salesman in California for the auto industry. Harlan Twible became CEO of a global manufacturing company. Jack Cassidy worked as a state policeman in Massachusetts.

Bob Gause returned to Florida as a commercial fisherman. (His sideline exploits as a shark hunter are said by some to have served as inspiration for the Captain Quint character in *Jaws*.) Whatever had happened to them on the water was in the past. They moved into the stream of America, and they *worked*.

Dr. Haynes went on to a successful career in military medicine, even serving in Vietnam, before leaving the service in 1965. Haynes retired to a town outside Boston. However, he was still troubled by nightmares of the sinking and found it difficult to attend church.

"Every church I go to recites the Lord's Prayer," he explained. "And every time I say the prayer, I still cry."

Private McCoy became a chiropractor in Missouri. He earned

a doctor of osteopathy degree, and devoted his life to helping other people.

One day in 1958, McCoy heard a knock at the front door of his home in Boonville, Missouri. On the porch he found one of his raft mates whose lives he and Bob Brundige had tried so hard to save. Since the sinking, Felton Outland had been thinking of the man who had helped keep him alive.

On impulse, Felton had just driven the nine hundred miles from his family's farm in Sunbury, North Carolina, to thank Private McCoy for his life. The two men stared at each other. Then they embraced and began weeping on the porch. They ended up talking for two days, a flood of memories pouring forth between them.

After Felton left, McCoy found himself moved by Outland's gratitude. Armed with the survivors' list published in Richard Newcomb's book, *Abandon Ship!*, he began trying to locate his former shipmates. He decided he wanted to organize a reunion of the men of the USS *Indianapolis*.

Many of the survivors wrote McCoy back, angry that he was dredging up memories long buried. McCoy himself was troubled by nightmares. But encouraged by a psychiatrist he had approached for advice about organizing the reunion, McCoy managed to find 220 of the original 316 survivors.

In July 1960, they met for the first time in fifteen years at a hotel in downtown Indianapolis. The reunion turned out to be a scorching experience.

The survivors unloaded years of repressed fear and anger.

They even discussed the shame of bad deeds, the smoldering guilt of having been unable to keep someone alive.

For many of the men, their survival at sea still felt like a miracle rather than a triumph of will over insurmountable odds and death.

They talked for hours, arranged in assigned seats that re-created the groups they had floated with across the Philippine Sea. The men emerged from the reunion gray-faced and drained, but liberated. McCoy felt a bond with these men that he knew he would never experience with anyone else.

~

After the court-martial, McVay had been reassigned to the naval air station outside New Orleans. Far from the glamour of life on the high seas, he was given a desk job. Still, he worked hard at tilting his life back toward some shade of its former happiness.

He and his wife, Louise, lived in a comfortable house on Fourth Street. The two were regular guests at parties that often ended with the captain standing at a piano singing. This was followed by the lighthearted retelling of stories about life in the navy. On weekends, the couple camped in a tidy shack on Bayou Liberty, north of New Orleans, and spent hours fishing for speckled trout.

In 1949, after thirty years of military service, McVay retired and began selling insurance. For the first time in his adult life, he was a civilian.

McVay attended the first survivors' reunion in 1960. On the plane ride to Indianapolis he was filled with worry and doubts. He'd spent the last fifteen years wondering if his former crew held him responsible for the disaster. He was shocked to tears when he stepped from the plane with Louise and found the survivors lining the airport's runway. All of his sailors were saluting, tears streaming down their own faces.

McCoy hadn't seen the captain since those moments back in the navy yard courtroom when he had testified on his behalf. In court, when McCoy had finished speaking, McVay had simply raised a finger and winked: *Thanks*.

Now, over drinks in McCoy's hotel room, McCoy told him, "Captain, you got a raw deal. And I want to do something about it. I'd like to see if we can get your name cleared."

The captain mulled this over and then his face darkened.

"No, that's all right, McCoy," he said. "I got what the regulations called for—I got what I deserved."

When the reunion was over, the men gathered on the hotel roof. They cheered and saluted the captain as his car pulled away for the airport. It was the last time they ever saw him.

Back at home, McVay began a slow spiral into despair. Louise was diagnosed with cancer and died suddenly in 1961. After years of self-restraint, he began to fall apart.

Within a year, he impulsively married Vivian Smith,

someone he had known during his youth. They moved to a farm in Litchfield, Connecticut. There were some happy times involving travel and hosting parties at the farm. But then in 1965, Captain McVay received what must have been a final blow. His grandson, in whom he had taken a special interest, died from a sudden illness.

McVay took to spending his days quietly, often alone. He puttered in a workshop building furniture, or played bridge, or rowed a blue boat around a small pond he'd dug on the property. One morning his stepson, Winthrop Smith Jr. (from Vivian's previous marriage), paused before the bathroom door in the Litchfield farmhouse and heard the captain weeping.

When he opened the door, he saw McVay, dressed in his khaki naval clothes. He was clutching a letter—more hate mail from the families of dead sailors. He told the young boy, "*I can't take this.*"

Not long after, on a cold November morning in 1968, Captain Charles Butler McVay III took his own life.

After the cremation, a memorial service was held in Arlington National Cemetery, complete with a twenty-one-gun salute. His remains were flown to Louisiana, where he'd spent the happiest times of his life.

If you'd been standing on the beach at Bayou Liberty that winter in 1968, you might have seen a plane pass by overhead. You might have seen the door open and a small box tipped to the wind. The contents went scattering, like a twisting scarf of smoke.

A man's bones and skin can be burned away into powder and ash, but what's left is without form. Courage, duty, and honor have no permanent home.

What was left of Charles Butler McVay melted on the water and was gone.

A NOTE FROM DOUG STANTON

Twenty-eight years after Captain McVay's death, in 1996, the U.S. Navy's Judge Advocate General delivered this pronouncement: "The conclusion reached is that Captain McVay's court-martial was legally sound; no injustice has been done, and remedial action is not warranted."

Over the years, conspiracy theories had waxed and waned among some survivors as they tried to explain why Captain McVay was court-martialed. Some believed Admiral King was seeking revenge for a personal insult allegedly inflicted years earlier by McVay's father. Still others believed the politically powerful father of one dead crew member successfully lobbied President Truman himself to press ahead with the trial. Ultimately, though, these theories added up to little.

The court-martial's effect was the ruin of McVay's career, and what remains today is the question of whether this was just.

In the years since the sinking, many of the survivors of the disaster worked tirelessly to clear their captain's name.

"The *Indianapolis* was a trim, fighting ship," said Dr. Haynes, "and I would be proud to serve aboard her once again." Or, as Bob Brundige, a former raft mate, once said, "We would've rode to hell with Captain McVay."

~

As it turned out, justice in the case of Captain Charles Butler McVay arrived on July 13, 2001—fifty-six years after the sinking of the ship. The Department of the Navy, in a surprising turn of events, made public their decision to exonerate the court-martialed captain.

Secretary of the Navy Gordon R. England instructed that the following declaration be appended to McVay's military service record: "The American people should now recognize Captain McVay's lack of culpability for the tragic loss of the USS *Indianapolis* and the lives of the men who died as a result of the sinking of that vessel."

What, after all these years, prompted the navy to reverse its decision fifty-six years after the court-martial?

In short, it was the result of dogged optimism and persistence on the part of hundreds of individuals.

~

The story of the USS *Indianapolis*, like the sea into which it disappeared on July 30, 1945, continues to offer up discoveries.[1] For example, in 2018, crew and casualty numbers were adjusted to account for a long-time error in the ship's sailing list, making the final tally of survivors 316 men.

On August 19, 2017, an expedition financed by explorer and philanthropist Paul Allen, and led by expedition director Robert Kraft, discovered the USS *Indianapolis* lying on the bottom of the Pacific Ocean, in 18,044 feet of water. The crystalline pictures and video sent back by the expedition's remote cameras revealed a ship practically preserved in time after seventy-two years of resting in cold darkness.

Today, the ship's exact location remains protected and is considered a grave site. But its remarkable discovery allows the crew and families, of those who'd survived and those who were lost at sea, to know that its final destination was no longer a mirage.

In July 2020, the crew was honored with the Congressional Gold Medal, Congress's highest honor. This was a well-deserved public proclamation of not only the crew's humble heroism but also of its hard and critical battle service.

More recognition of the crew followed when, on January 8,

---

1 See "Setting the Record Straight: Loss of the USS *Indianapolis* and the Question of Clarence Donnor," by Richard Hulver and Sara Vladic, *Proceedings,* March 2018.

2021, then-Secretary of the Navy Kenneth Braithwaite posthumously honored Father Thomas Conway, the ship's chaplain, with the Navy Cross.

The ceremony capped a years-long effort begun, in some respect, by Dr. Lewis Haynes after his rescue, to memorialize the selfless sacrifice of his friend who perished tending to shipmates. In 2013, retired navy chaplain Father John Bevins had read *In Harm's Way* and was inspired to launch an advocacy campaign for the award.

The 2020 reunion highlighted the twenty-eight African Americans who served aboard the *Indianapolis* and did not survive the ordeal. Until recently, their stories have gone largely untold.

Among the twenty-eight sailors was Magellan Williams, Steward's Mate 1C, from Downsville, Louisiana, who was twenty-one when he went down with the ship. Clarence Sims, Cook 2C, from Henning, Tennessee, served as Captain McVay's valet and had been aboard for nearly four years when he was lost at sea. Henry Jackson, Steward's Mate 1C, was thirty-eight years old, from Beaverdam, Virginia, and had been aboard a little over a year. Also aboard was Albert Rice, Steward's Mate 1C, age twenty, from Kansas City, Kansas, who'd joined the ship in April 1944.

The ship that sailed from California on July 16, 1945, was a mirror of the segregated country it left behind, a floating city where sailors were literally compartmentalized in differing worlds based on rank and race. President Harry Truman would finally desegregate the navy on July 26, 1948 (though desegregation was not immediate), and it would be nearly sixteen years before the Civil Rights Act of 1964 was passed by President Lyndon Johnson, on July 2, 1964.

"Life was hard on all enlisted men in a navy ship in World War II," says Sandra Gall, formerly of the Naval History and Heritage Command. "Living conditions [were] rough, though not hard to imagine it was tougher for African Americans, who faced racism from white crew members and worked as cooks, stewards, etc., which were seen as lower-status jobs among navy ratings."

The twenty-eight African American sailors aboard the *Indy* were bunked in a forward area where the torpedoes smashed into the hull. It's impossible to determine how many survived the explosions and made it into the water.

~

African American crew members were not the only group aboard the ship who faced discrimination and whose roles went unacknowledged until recently.

In 2013, Adolfo "Harpo" Celaya explained to the Veterans History Project that he'd seen more than one poster around his hometown, Florence, Arizona, promising that navy men got to see the world. Harpo was seventeen, too young by law to join without his father's signature. The elder Celaya reluctantly agreed.

When the ship sunk, Harpo, adrift in the sea, discovered that he was not welcomed aboard a raft. "I was going to get on [one] but some of the guys that were on there wouldn't allow me to. I grabbed hold of some rope, and I stayed there."

"My friend, Santos Pena, said the same thing happened to him. [Santos] got up to a raft and there were two or three guys on there, they told him to get away."

In 2020, in *Smithsonian* magazine, Celaya explained that during the survivors' return trip to the U.S. aboard an aircraft carrier after their rescue, and during which they were convalescing, he was tasked to work detail three days in a row, despite his exhaustion after five days adrift at sea. Celaya explained that "any jobs that were not taken by a white person would be given down to anybody that had Hispanic blood."

When he complained to an officer, he was thrown in solitary confinement and fed nothing but bread and water for two days. Celaya told the Veteran's History Project, "It was kind of rough for me, I mean, that my country would do that to me."

Celaya re-engaged with his shipmates in the early 1970s, at the urging of rescue pilot Chuck Gwinn, with whom he'd become close friends. At Gwinn's patient urging, Celaya would finally break a long silence and begin speaking to school students about his navy experience. But the wounds he suffered remained fresh years later, and he didn't attempt to attend another reunion until 2019, an effort, unfortunately, thwarted by illness, but which opened a path of re-engagement in 2020 when Celaya, with his shipmates, participated (virtually) in the Congressional Gold Medal award ceremony.

In discussing how to talk about the ship's history, and about people of color who served aboard the *Indy*, Dr. Jeannette Pitts, niece of lost-at-sea Steward's Mate Albert Rice, explained: "I want these men's memory to be honored, their lives to be honored, their sacrifice to be recognized, to realize that they had the same dreams and hopes that others did, that they had the same, if not more, hardships. They had families that they left behind, and there are repercussions and impacts through the generations for these families, talents and skills that were lost, children that were unborn."

Within a generation, some of the only people left to tell the story of the *Indianapolis* will be the descendants of those who survived and did not survive the sinking. And because far more did not survive, this latter group likely represents a broader spectrum of race and class in mid-century America. Collecting these oral histories of African American sailors is a new, and long-overdue, page in the USS *Indianapolis* story. To read more, see www.ussindianapolis.org.

In a story filled with many twists, one of the most persistent is whether or not anyone on shore received a distress message from the *Indianapolis* as it sank. The Naval History and Heritage Command concluded, as the navy had argued during Captain

McVay's 1945 court-martial, that no SOS left the ship and, therefore, none was received onshore.

In the 2001 edition of *In Harm's Way*, I cite three individuals who believe they witnessed receipt of an SOS message from the *Indy*; two of them testified at a 1999 hearing before the Committee on Armed Services. When I asked *Indianapolis* survivor Dick Thelen recently if he believes a message was sent, he said he did. In my interview with Radioman Jack Miner, he believed the same. Of course, "believing" doesn't make a fact. What's curious is the persistence of recollections by sailors who believe such a message was sent, and that it was not acted upon.

The court-martial of Captain McVay commenced some five months after the sinking. It's possible that message traffic of July 30, 1945, received four days before the men were accidentally discovered, was preserved by someone in the immediate aftermath, but hard-copy evidence has not emerged.

Whether or not a message was received "has probably been the most vexing question of the sad saga," says Rear Admiral (retired) Samuel Cox. "Our historians have given it their best shot, although I am not convinced there will ever be a definitive answer to this question."

Traverse City, Michigan
July 2021

THE USS
*INDIANAPOLIS/*GWINN
"ANGEL" SCHOLARSHIP

In June 2002, Doug Stanton, author of *In Harm's Way*, conceived of and funded the USS *Indianapolis* Survivors Fund Scholarship Program to benefit family members of the ship's crew and help preserve the *Indy*'s historic legacy. In 2008, the fund was permanently endowed by the family of Wilbur C. Gwinn as the USS *Indianapolis/*Gwinn "Angel" Scholarship. Gwinn was the pilot who first spotted the survivors and initiated their rescue at sea.

The purpose of the scholarship is to preserve the stories of the ship and its crew. Prospective and continuing college students are encouraged to research the story of the USS *Indianapolis* CA-35 and write about their own families.

The scholarship is open to descendants (including stepchildren) of USS *Indianapolis* CA-35 crew members involved in the tragedy—its survivors, lost at sea (LAS), rescue and recovery crew, and those who have merited honorary survivor status by the Survivors Organization. For information, see https://gtrcf .academicworks.com/opportunities/895.

GLOSSARY

Aft: toward the stern of a vessel

Axis powers: Germany, Italy, and Japan, which were allied before and during World War II

Ballast: material to supply stability to a ship. Water can be moved into a ballast tank to provide balance on a ship.

Battleship: a large, armed warship with many deck guns

Blip (on a radar screen): a light or spot on the radar screen indicating an object has been detected

Bridge: a room on a platform where the ship can be commanded

Bombardier: a member of an aircraft crew responsible for releasing bombs

Bow: the front of the vessel

Bulkhead: an upright wall within the hull of the ship

CINCPAC: In World War II, this referred to the headquarters of naval operation in the Pacific or Commander in Chief, Pacific Fleet.

Court-martial: a judicial court for trying members of the armed services accused of an offense against military law

Destroyer: a small, fast warship

Dogging hatches: to close the hatches. Hatches are like doors on a ship, separating compartments.

Flotilla: a fleet of ships

Fuselage: the central body portion of an aircraft

Hatch: an opening or small door on a ship

Head: the ship's toilet area. The name originally came from the days when the toilets were located near the bow.

Hull: the watertight structure of the vessel

Keening: wailing in grief

Knot: a nautical term used as a unit of speed, approximately 1.15 miles per hour

Keel: the bottom-most structure around the hull. It runs along the centerline of the ship from the bow to the stern. The keel adds stability to the vessel.

Life ring: a doughnut-shaped flotation device

List: the degree to which a vessel leans or tilts to either the starboard or port side

Monkey fist: a large heavy knot at the end of a line to weight the end and assist when throwing. Sometimes a weight is attached to the end of the line.

PBY: The U.S. Navy designation for a specific amphibious aircraft. The PB stands for Patrol Bomber, and Y is the code assigned to Consolidated Aircraft as its manufacturer.

Periscope (on a submarine): a tube attached to a set of mirrors that can be raised from the submerged submarine to scan the ocean's surface

Port: the left side of the vessel

Quartermaster: an officer who specializes in navigation

Radio shack: structure that houses radio equipment

Recon and reconnaissance: observation of a region to locate an enemy or strategic features

Reveille: a signal sound to wake personnel of the armed forces. Usually using a bugle or drum.

Sonar gear: equipment used to generate and receive sound. Usually to detect objects on or under the surface of water.

Starboard: the right side of the vessel

Steaming: informal term for a ship's movement

Stern: the back of the vessel

Taps: the last bugle call at night, blown as a signal that lights are to be put out

ULTRA: an Allied intelligence project that decoded encrypted communications from the Axis powers

Wardroom: the space on a warship for the living quarters of the officers (with the exception of the captain who has his own room)

Wings on a ship: A bridgewing is a narrow walkway extending from both sides of the pilothouse to the full width of the ship.

Zigzagging: an evasive maneuver used by a ship to avoid being hit by a torpedo. Rather than go in a straight line the ship moves forward by turning frequently at angles.

MICHAEL J. TOUGIAS'S BOOKS

New York Times–bestselling author Michael Tougias has earned critical acclaim for his narrative nonfiction. His books honor real-life, everyday people who rise to face life-threatening situations, make heroic choices, and survive against all odds. Several of his books have been adapted into the True Rescue series, including *The Finest Hours, A Storm Too Soon, Attacked at Sea, Into the Blizzard,* and *Rescue of the Bounty.*

His books for adults include:

Rescue of the Bounty: Disaster and Survival in Superstorm Sandy, co-author Douglas Campbell

A Storm Too Soon: A True Story of Disaster, Survival, and an Incredible Rescue

Overboard! A True Blue-Water Odyssey of Disaster and Survival

Fatal Forecast: An Incredible True Tale of
Disaster and Survival at Sea

Ten Hours Until Dawn: The True Story of
Heroism and Tragedy Aboard the Can Do

The Finest Hours: The True Story of the U.S. Coast Guard's
Most Daring Sea Rescue, co-author Casey Sherman

King Philip's War: The History and Legacy of America's
Forgotten Conflict, co-author Eric Schultz

Above and Beyond: John F. Kennedy and America's Most
Dangerous Cold War Spy Mission, co-author Casey Sherman

There's a Porcupine in My Outhouse: The Vermont
Misadventures of a Mountain Man Wannabe

So Close to Home: A True Story of an American Family's Fight
for Survival During World War II, co-author Alison O'Leary

BIBLIOGRAPHY

Clemans, Charles. *Harpo: War Survivor, Basketball Wizard.* Tuscon, AZ: Wheatmark, 2009.

Hashimoto, Mochitsura. *Sunk!: The Story of the Japanese Submarine Fleet, 1942–1945.* New York: Henry Holt, 1954.

Helm, Thomas. *Ordeal by Sea: The Tragedy of the U.S.S.* Indianapolis. New York: Dodd, Mead and Co., 1963.

Hulver, Richard; Luebke, Peter, associate editor. *A Grave Misfortune: The USS* Indianapolis *Tragedy.* Washington, D.C.: Naval History and Heritage Command, Department of the Navy, 2018.

Kurzman, Dan. *Fatal Voyage: The Sinking of the USS* Indianapolis. New York: Atheneum, 1990.

Lech, Raymond B. *All the Drowned Sailors.* New York: Stein and Day, 1982.

Moore, Katherine D. *Goodbye Indy Maru.* Knoxville, TN: Lori Publications, 1991.

Newcomb, Richard F. *Abandon Ship!: Death of the USS* Indianapolis. New York: Henry Holt, 1958.

Solly, Meilan. "See 12 Stunning Portraits of World War II Veterans," www.smithsonianmag.com. August 2019.

USS *Indianapolis* Survivors. *Only 317 Survived!: USS* Indianapolis *CA–35— Navy's Worst Tragedy at Sea.* Indianapolis: Printing Partners, 2002

Wren, L. Peter. *Those in Peril on the Sea.* Richmond, VA: L. Peter Wren, 1999.

Vincent, Lynn; Vladic, Sara. Indianapolis: *The True Story of the Worst Sea Disaster in U.S. Naval History and the Fifty-Year Fight to Exonerate an Innocent Man.* New York: Simon and Schuster, 2018.

DOUG STANTON is a #1 *New York Times*–bestselling author whose writing has appeared in *Esquire*, the *New York Times*, *TIME*, the *Washington Post*, and other national publications. The bestselling *In Harm's Way* was included in the US Navy's required reading list for naval officers. His book *Horse Soldiers* is the basis for the movie *12 Strong*, starring Chris Hemsworth. Stanton lectures nationally and has appeared on national TV and radio. He and his wife, Anne Stanton, provided an initial donation for the publication of *Only 316 Survived* and founded a scholarship program benefiting grandchildren of the USS *Indianapolis* crew at www.gtrcf.org/give/our-funds.html/159/.

DOUGSTANTON.COM

MICHAEL J. TOUGIAS is the author of many award-winning true rescue stories, including the *New York Times* bestseller *The Finest Hours*, *A Storm Too Soon*, *Into the Blizzard*, *Attacked at Sea*, and *Abandon Ship!* His recent books include *Extreme Survival: Lessons from Those Who Have Triumphed Against All Odds* and *The Waters Between Us: A Boy, a Father, Outdoor Misadventures, and the Healing Power of Nature*. A frequent lecturer on his work, Tougias splits his time between Massachusetts and Florida.

MICHAELTOUGIAS.COM

DON'T MISS THESE OTHER
TRUE RESCUE STORIES

A STORM
TOO SOON

A REMARKABLE TRUE SURVIVAL
STORY IN 80 FOOT SEAS

THE FINEST HOURS
THE TRUE STORY OF A HEROIC

MICHAEL J. TOUGIAS & CASE

AEL J. TOUGIAS

ATTACKED
AT SEA
A TRUE WORLD WAR II STORY OF A
FAMILY'S FIGHT FOR SURVIVAL
TRUE RESCUE SERIES

INTO THE
BLIZZARD
HEROISM AT SEA DURING THE
GREAT BLIZZARD OF 1978
TRUE RESCUE SERIES

NEW YORK TIMES BESTSELLING AUTHOR
MICHAEL J. TOUGIAS

An adaptation for young readers of Ten Hours Until Dawn:
The True Story of Heroism and Tragedy Aboard the Can Do

RESCUE OF THE
BOUNTY
DISASTER AND SURVIVAL IN
SUPERSTORM SANDY

TRUE RESCUE SERIES

MICHAEL J. TOUGIAS AND
DOUGLAS A. CAMPBELL